To Ride a Magic Carpet

George W. Braswell, Jr.

Broadman Press
Nashville, Tennessee

© Copyright 1977 • Broadman Press
All rights reserved.
4263-08
ISBN: 0-8054-6308-9

Dewey Decimal Classification: 266.55
Subject heading: MISSIONS—IRAN // IRAN

Library of Congress Catalog Card Number: 77-78472
Printed in the United States of America

Foreword

This book is a fascinating account of experiences—many of them unique—among Iranian Muslims, by a man who knew what to look for and how to interpret what he saw.

George Braswell and his wife Joan were the first Southern Baptist missionaries to Iran. They were just the right persons for the job. Cultured, friendly, established in their own faith but tolerant and understanding of others, they quickly adapted to the Iranian culture and formed wide-ranging and meaningful friendships.

Presbyterians and Anglicans, who have a long and noble missionary history in Iran, were cordial and helpful. George was determined that whatever he might do would add strength to the total Christian cause. He worked part-time in a Presbyterian language and culture center. A Presbyterian missionary helped him secure a position teaching English and Comparative Religions to Muslim theological students in the University of Tehran. For a while he taught in a girls' college which was formerly sponsored by Presbyterians.

Think of a missionary teaching daughters of prominent Muslim Iranians and young men who were preparing to be teachers of Islam. What knowledge and tact were needed! What doors could be—and were—opened by students, their relatives, and colleagues! What opportunities for Muslim-Christian dialogue and witness!

In 1969 George was largely responsible for the program of a Middle East Baptist missionaries' conference in Tehran on Christian Missions among Muslims. He had already established friendships which enabled him to bring in outstanding guest speakers, some of them Christians who had been brought up as Muslims. The conference focused on the Christian Message to Muslims and Missionary Methods among Muslims. Again and again we were reminded that we must know Islam and Muslims if our message and our methods are to be right.

Braswell knows Islam, and he knows Muslims. The Iranians are Shiite Muslims. Their special beliefs and practices are presented inductively through varied experiences which the author had with them.

This is not a book of missionary "success stories." It is about dialogue—with those on each side, convinced of their own heritage, respectful of those on the other side, and willing to learn. It also reveals proclamation and shows how the way was prepared for future proclamation. It is a good background book on Iran, Islam, and missions.

I applauded George's decision to interrupt his promising missionary career for studies of Anthropology and Missions, and I was awed by his ability to earn a university doctorate and a seminary doctorate at the same time. My emotions were mixed when he and his wife offered their resignation as foreign missionaries so he could become a member of the faculty of Southeastern Baptist Theological Seminary. There was sadness because of the loss for Iran and joy because of the gain for American theological (and missionary) education. In one way or another the Braswells will doubtless continue what they began in Iran.

I hope each reader will find the book as readable and informative as I have.

J. D. HUGHEY
Secretary for Europe, the Middle East, and South Asia
Southern Baptist Foreign Mission Board

Preface

Persons make things happen. This is a brief story about persons from the western world and the middle eastern world in touch with one another. Persons also project the possible and provide the power and the perseverance to see the completion of the task. This book affirms my belief in and reliance upon persons. They enabled a missionary-anthropologist to immerse himself in the lives of Iranian people.

Some of these persons are local church folk who planted in me the thirst for knowledge and the sharing of faith and belief of a life's pilgrimage. Some are mission agency folk who risked me in the Muslim world to work with the possible. Others are academician persons who wanted me to wrestle clues from the mysteries of another people and culture. And there are those who are the actors and actresses deep in their home territory of Iran. These latter individuals, anonymous as they are in name, provided the life substance for these pages. Their flesh and blood embroider the mosaic of this Persian carpet stitching, and sometimes the stitching comes unraveled.

And there are those persons who are most warm flesh to me. My wife, Joan, and my children, Margaret Anne, Robbie, Brien, and Becky walked some exciting and exotic and demanding pathways with me in Iran. They were in-the-flesh encouragers, sustainers, challengers, and willing riders of magic carpets. To them I dedicate this book.

So I thank all for words of encouragement, of provisions of sustenance along the way, of generous gifts of affirmation of work and purpose, and of all the cups of Iranian tea, rice, and meat pilous, and Persian carpets upon which to sit and endlessly chat. Iranian hospitality is singularly rich.

Now come with me and ride a magic carpet.

CONTENTS

Introduction

Kings, Cats, Carpets, and Church

1	You Gotta Know the Territory	15
2	Tea for Two and More	21
3	The Unveiling	36
4	A Young Man Beats His Drum	55
5	The Stillness of the Wind	70
6	A Season of Obedience	87
7	God, King, and Country	111
8	And the Beat Goes On	134

Introduction

Kings, Cats, Carpets, and Church

King of kings! Shahenshah! What a title to be called. And in October, 1967, the Shah of Iran was allowing himself and his queen to be crowned in the grandeur of 2,500 years of royal lineage. He was proud to announce to the world that Iran, old Persia, had become of age. The Shah had ruled as king since 1941, but he felt his country had remained in the Dark Ages. With his reliance upon the support of the Western world, he had brought old Persia a long way. Now was his time to usher Iran into the world of great nations.

In that same fall of 1967, my family and I were in orientation sessions in preparation to become the first representatives of the Foreign Mission Board of the Southern Baptist Convention to Iran. Historically, Iran was not a foreign country to me. As a young lad, Sunday School teachers used to signal out King Cyrus of ancient Persia as one of the greatest figures in world history. Had not the book of Isaiah of the Old Testament referred to him as the messiah of God? King Cyrus had liberated the Jews from their Babylonian captivity and had given them a homeland in Persia. I had learned from Sunday School teachers and the Old Testament that Persian Kings, like Darius and Artaxerxes, encouraged and supported the Jews in the rebuilding of the Jerusalem Temple. To my growing mind, those Persian kings were larger than life and were to be further examined in their positions as Shahenshahs.

My early world of learning was filled with other Persian figures and symbols. Esther of Old Testament renown was queen to a Shahenshah. She intervened with her consort to preserve her Jewish people from destruction. Ezra, Nehemiah, and Daniel, in Bible stories taught to me, described the benevolences of the Persian peoples. And my teachers used to exclaim over the good sight and tenacious perseverance of the Magi, the priests of Persia, as they faithfully followed the star over the Mesopotamian deserts to the village of Bethlehem. Their gifts, laid at the feet of the little Babe, depicted an intense loyalty and expectation in the newborn child. I often wondered why the Magi didn't cast aside their camels for a carpet and ride the mountainous wind currents to the south of Palestine. And why didn't they offer the Babe a Persian cat, for that was an elite symbol in my early upbringing. After all, could not a king of kings and a wise man do what they willed?

From my early years I had an interest in old Persia, and moved into a steady stream of immersion into Persian kings, peoples, and religions in my graduate school days. Kings and church took precedence in my attention over Persian cats and carpets. I began to call Persia, Iran, and the Persian people, Iranians. After serious study I learned of the near-takeover of the known world by the Shahenshahs between the sixth and third centuries B.C. Later, when I was in language study in Iran, I often secretly wished that the Persians had done just that, so that Persian would have become the lingua franca. I began to appreciate the Magi as priests of the Zoroastrian religion, that faith of light and good deeds, which claimed the loyalties of Iranians from the time of King Cyrus to the Islamic invasion. And the little Babe! The Christian church was introduced to Iran soon after the development of the early church in Palestine, and the ancient church of the East became the early fountain of Christian witness in ancient Persia.

Another phenomenon also captured my interest. Islam, the religion founded and propagated by the prophet Mohammed, emerged out of the Saudi Arabian peninsula in the seventh century A.D., and soon thereafter encompassed the entirety of Iran. The swift capitulation of Iran to the Islamic religion intrigued me. The brand of Iranian Islam was Shiism, a religion that centered on hero types who were charismatic in leadership and were carriers of the divine light. Iranian Muslims, or Shiites, identified in vicarious suffering in the death of their prophets. Jesus Christ, too, was considered by Shiites to be a prophet.

Beyond my school days, the mystery of old and new Persia haunted me. In October, 1967, at the very time the Shahenshah of Iran was proclaiming a new era among his countrymen, my family and I were about to launch into new Persia. But I was soon to learn that Iran was much more than the land of kings, cats, carpets, and church.

During the years 1968–1974, my family and I lived in Iran, except for a home leave back to the United States. For three years I was the only Westerner on the faculty of Islamic theology of the University of Tehran, a seminary of some six hundred students. At the University of Tehran I also taught English and comparative religions. At Damavand College, a girl's college of six hundred students, I introduced sociology and anthropology into the curriculum. Along with these assignments, I helped my Presbyterian colleagues with the administration duties of Armaghan Institute, an English language and cultural center, which enrolled some five hundred students yearly. But above all, my daily vocation involved me with Iranians in their homes, mosques, temples, churches, streets, shops, cities, towns and villages, and in their work.

The story I wish to tell in these pages, is my experiences with Iranians on their home turf. However, in reading the story one should note my reasons for journeying to and in Iran. My family and I packed our bags and set out for Iran as Christians on a mission. Iran classifies some ninety-eight percent of its inhabitants as Muslims. How does one approach this monolithic Muslim world? I approached that world with certain presuppositions and commitments, having been nurtured in the church and shaped by Christian education.

I entered Iran as a Christian from the West, as a recipient of the good news that God was in Christ reconciling the world unto himself. I am conditioned by the life, teachings, death, and resurrection of Jesus Christ. I have been raised in the life of the church, and have been persuaded through preaching, teaching, and the winds of the Spirit to affirm the truth which is in Jesus Christ. The decisions of early church councils, the Crusades, the Inquisition, the Reformation, the modern missionary movement, the near silence of the church in the great social issues of the day, the "post-Christian" era in the West, secularism, and the revival of the great religions, continually lend their influences upon my reflections and being in the world, and these decisions color other's attitudes and relationships toward me.

I went as a Christian. Jesus Christ said, "As I am sent, so I send you." I did not presume that I was sent into a vacuum. Do we not recall that in the great land of Persia that God called King Cyrus, his anointed, to do his will? The Spirit confronts Iranian rulers and peoples with the search for the truth. The Spirit is present in the lives of Iranian Christians. The Spirit has already come; it has been sent. But I was sent. I was sent with a Word which is more than a word. I was sent by the one who shaped my being sent. The Word became a human being and lived among us, for us, in spite of us. I do not have the final word. He is the Word. I do not possess the ultimate truth. He is the truth. I do not hold the only way. He is the way.

And what about the message which I bear? Word is event. God is in Christ. Speech is action. Wherever I am sent, something is happening. It is true that I groan, others groan, the whole created order groans for a new creation. We want to sit around a table, or at least face one another, not behind walls or with heads turned. The message comes as truth is presented through personality centered in Christ, as life and energy of vocation meets a genuine need in the life of the people to whom one is sent, as the love of God is enacted in understanding the human journey and in making available the resources both of the Spirit and of matter to make life more personal, abundant, sane, and whole.

And I am a Christian from the West. This is as much a given as my being a Christian. Not only is my Trinitarian concept misunderstood by those of the Muslim world, but also the sectarian, denominational groupings to which I conform are puzzling. The coloration given to the preaching of the gospel and adherence to its teachings by social and economic classes of Christians raise questions of validity. The church's prolonged silence on the great human experiences of suffering and death, in the areas of famine, race, and war, has caused the missionary message to be viewed with suspicion. Theological positions which distinguish sharply between the clean and the unclean, the savage and the civilized, the pagan and the God-favored have often sounded like pronouncements of superiority. The wealth of the church in displaying both quantity of talent, money, materials, advice, rules and orders, and expertise in the "subjugated land" as well as having the home front racing at top speed to keep the dollars and personnel flowing in, has tended to both compromise the message and to restrict the messenger.

With our good life of material abundance, with our techniques for building and destroying, with our basic unfamiliarity and sometime subtle suspicions of different peoples and cultures, we find ourselves misunderstanding and misunderstood.

And to whom was I sent? The Muslim world and Muslims! I went to a people with an established, historic, world religion. I went to a cultured people of Islam with their law, science, and life, reflecting deep religious values. I went to a people who remember the clash of their religion with the Christian religion—of the East with the West. I spoke with a people who adhere to the religion of Abraham, who refer to Jesus in the Qur'an with more titles of honor than any other figure, including their prophet, Mohammed. They call themselves the People of the Book, along with the Zoroastrians, Jews, and Christians. They take history seriously, and look forward to the coming of the Messiah (a Shiite prophetic figure, and Mehdi).

I journeyed to Iran believing that the Christian message enables the one sent to understand those to whom he is sent. He is enabled to see where the Spirit is at work, to sense the needs, to shape the proper response, and to get on with his vocational task. The message of the Christian neither causes one to be in judgment upon the people themselves, nor does it make of one a defender of faith, but it liberates one to be an interpreter of the truth, to be a friend and neighbor to those around one, and to engage in the ministry of reconciliation as one validly participates in the life and work of the society.

What started out in my experience as a fascination with old Persia rapidly was translated into a commitment to understand and communicate with new Iran. As the story unfolds, it is my hope that a mosaic of the lives of Iranians may emerge which places kings, cats, and carpets in their proper places.

1 You Gotta Know the Territory

The first day in Iran is like your last day, especially as you cross the narrow streets. The secret to survival is to rapidly learn the territory. Villagers in their bare feet have learned it to perfection. Donkeys and sheep and goats parade in the streets having learned the secret genetically, I suppose. But for a foreigner from America who knows a lot of history about the building of streets and viaducts, but little about the Iranian streets themselves, the lesson of learning the territory becomes a Darwinian necessity in the survival of the fittest. You cross the street with abandon, just as other pedestrians, sheep, goats, cart-pushers, and blind singers, do. Somehow, you wind and weave through the stream of cars, trucks, bicycles, and motorized scooters, and you usually arrive on the other side to experience your salvation. The secret, of course and always, is to know the territory.

Iran is like the street scene. I began to see through and beyond the cultural haze when I dared to take the risk and mix with the surrounding environment. The first gem I learned to perfection was to step out into the street. Through pushing, shoving, being pushed and shoved; following, leading, not looking, holding on, and feeling the bumpers of cars pressing my flesh, I began to feel a little at ease in my adopted home. But there is more to the territory than the street crossing.

Iran lies in southwestern Asia and is bound to the north by Russia, to the south by the oil-rich Persian Gulf, to the west by Turkey and Iraq, and to the east by Afghanistan and West Pakistan. Iran's history is long, and her present Shahenshah is described as being a part of the royal lineage of five hundred kings, belonging to forty dynasties, who reigned over Iran for some two thousand and five hundred years. However, over the years the stability of Iran has been challenged. The Greeks, the Arabs, and the Mongols have invaded the country and left their indelible marks upon Iran's heritage. In more recent times the great powers have used Iran as a pawn in their economic and political ambitions. Both Russia and England wielded influence in the country in the first half of this century, and divided the country into two spheres of influence which were mutually satisfying to their geopolitical needs.

In the last decade while growing rich from its vast oil resources, Iran has assumed an important place economically, politically, and militarily both in the Middle East and in the world arena. This rapid rise to power has caused some problems with her neighbors. Russia still remains a formidable threat to the Persian Gulf interests of Iran. Turkey has presented a strong challenge to Iranian kings in its secularization of Islam, which the kings have emulated. Afghanistan and West Pakistan have historically been under the influence of Persian rulers, and although these countries have been Muslim neighbors to Iran, uneasy tensions have existed from time to time. Iraq is the keeper of the great Shiite Islamic shrines located near Baghdad. Although Iran and Iraq make much of being "Muslim brothers," there have been deep differences over each nation's rights to the Persian Gulf, over the issue of the Kurds, and over Persian-Arab cultural differences. Iranian Shiites have often been denied the right to visit the Shiite shrines in Iraq.

Islam claims some ninety-eight percent of the population of Iran. However, the Zoroastrian religion antedates Islam by some one thousand years. Today, Zoroastrians have decreased to about fifty thousand adherents. Judaism, introduced into the country when King Cyrus freed the Jews from the Babylonian captivity, is represented sparsely. Bahaism, which arose in Iran in the nineteenth century, is considered an heretical religion by Iranian authorities, and little public knowledge of Iranian Bahaism is known.

Christianity is said to have entered Iran in the apostolic era in the form of the ancient church of the East, which later came to be known as "Nestorian." Today,. Christians number more than two hundred thousand and count in their numbers Assyrians, Armenians, both Roman Catholics and Protestants and Orthodox, the Episcopal Church of the Middle East (the Diocese of Iran, a child of Anglican missions), the Evangelical Church of Iran (a child of Presbyterian missionary efforts), and many other denominations and sects.

A major clue for understanding the Iranian, both in the street and in the home, is the religion, Islam. My children, in their younger days, always searched for M and M candy in Iran. It wasn't labeled M and M on the package, but they could buy a similar kind in the corner, grocery store. When I think of M and M candy, I think of four other Ms which give clues to the Iranian's religion. The mosque is the simple, bare structure, sometimes ornately decorated, but more often not, where Iranian Muslims go for worship and study and socializing. A mosque is usually located in every neighborhood.

The minaret is the slender, spiraling column which protrudes from the roof of the mosque toward the sky. It houses a stairway inside where the Muslim clergyman ascends to the top to call the people to prayer several times each day. More recently, electrified, audio systems have been installed in the minarets to sound the call to prayer. The mihrab is a visible notch in the wall of the large interior room of the mosque which signals the direction of the city of Mecca. It was in Mecca that the prophet Mohammed built a large worship center, and it is toward Mecca that worshiping Muslims bow in their prayers. The mambar is the elevated pulpit in the mosque which the Muslim preacher ascends to preach from the Muslim holy book, the Qur'an. Friday is the special day of worship in the mosque, but every day people attend the mosque for their prayers and for a brief sermon by the preacher.

A good Muslim is extremely conscious of at least two components of his religion, the six pillars of his faith and a strong sense of history. He confesses that he believes in one God whom he calls Allah and in Allah's chief spokesman, the prophet, Mohammed. He faithfully says his prayers five times daily, often in the mosque and frequently in the home or at work. He gives percentages of his wealth to the mosque. He fasts one month a year. If his health and finances allow, he makes a pilgrimage to the holy city of Mecca in Saudi Arabia once in his lifetime. And he is commissioned to witness for his faith.

The Iranian Muslim's sense of history is quite keen. He is called a Shiite which means a partisan. At the time of Mohammed's death the religion Islam had been well established in the central cities of Saudi Arabia. However, Mohammed had not prescribed any clear method for selecting a successor to himself. The early Muslim community chose certain men to act in the prophet's behalf. Mohammed's daughter, Fatima, had married Ali, the cousin of the prophet. Ali considered his claim to succeed the prophet as valid, for after all he was Mohammed's son-in-law. The short of the matter is that Ali and his sons, Hasan and Husain, became known as the Shiite branch of Islam, and claimed to be the legitimate representation of the prophet's rule.

The Shiite branch of Islam is founded upon the rule of twelve Imams (religious authorities), Ali and his sons being the first three Imams. Husain, the third Imam, has special meaning for Shiites, for he and his entire family of some eighty persons were massacred by the Sunni branch of Islam. Husain has become the prototype martyr, and Shiites in various kinds of ceremonies identify with him in vicarious suffering. Shiite tradition says that the twelfth Imam, the Mehdi, disappeared in the prime of his life and will return from his hidden state one day to set up a kingdom of right and good on the earth.

In the meantime, Shiites believe that their Muslim clergymen act in behalf of the Imams until the return of the Mehdi. This belief places a great deal of confidence and power in the hands of the clergy. Consequently, there is always ambivalence and tension in many areas of authority between the mosques and government. Shiite history in Iran is replete with conflict between Muslim clergy and the government. Therefore, the daily lives of Iranian Shiites are lived on a stage which is often preconditioned by the conflict between "church" and state. It is extremely helpful to know the territory of Islamic belief and practice in Iran, for it enables one to journey through the complex mazeways of people's lives in sensitivity and understanding.

Iran is rapidly becoming a land of cities and towns. Its thirty-five million people are rapidly becoming an urban population. Tehran, the capital, is located in the northern plateau at the foot of the Elburz Mountains. Its four million inhabitants represent a conglomerate of ethnic, religious, and economic samples of the population. My family and I settled into the exciting and exotic ways of Tehran life. The wide boulevards with grass medians and water fountains are the result of Reza Shah Pahlavi's ascension to the crown in 1925. The highways and railways that link the capital with Tabriz to the north, to Meshed to the east, and to Isfahan and Shiraz and Abadan to the south are also the outcome of Reza Shah Pahlavi's reign. Reza Shah, also known as the Father of Modernization in Iran, banned the wearing of the veil (chador) by Iranian women, and encouraged both women and men to wear Western dress. But fifty years have passed and women still wear the veil in public. They feel constrained to do so, but that is a story for later.

As a young lad, Mohammed Reza Shah Pahlavi succeeded his father in 1941 at a time when the allied forces occupied Iran. They were difficult times for the novice Shah, and it was really not until the decade of the sixties that he began to move Iran into the modern era. The Shah's palaces are located in Tehran, as well as all central bureaucracies of the government. The University of Tehran, established during the reign of Reza Shah with its twenty thousand students, stands behind gates in downtown Tehran. One sure sign of modernity is the two hundred movie houses scattered over the city, showing Western films on sex and violence for twenty-five cents admission. The international airport lies just to the west of the city, bringing in by jumbo jets thousands of Westerners eager to capitalize on Iran's new oil wealth.

But it is time now to get back into the streets where the people are. Not all the streets are wide avenues. In fact, most streets are alleyways, fondly called by Iranians as Kuchehs. The home, mosque, teahouse, and the drama of daily life is in the alleyways. But when one moves off the street, one passes beyond the wall into this other world. Once off the street, everything is behind walls. And often permission is difficult to gain to get behind those walls.

2 Tea for Two and More

The world of the mullah is an enigmatic one in Iran. The mullah is a Muslim clergyman who may lead daily prayers in the mosque, preach from the mambar, counsel his people in the intricacies of Islamic belief and practice, christen a young baby, and utter the final rites over the grave. But he is more. "Mr. Mullah" is a sign and a symbol for millions of Shiites of the promise and power of the agency of the Imams, particularly as he ministers to his people in their expectations of the return of the twelfth Imam.

The mullah is not easily accessible to a foreigner, for he mostly operates his daily activities within the walls of the mosque, the homes of the faithful, and his own dwelling. His dress is distinctive. He wears the turban, the flowing robe, sandals or slipper shoes which are easy to kick off, and a beard. He is constantly fingering beads, either for saying prayers or exerting nervous energy. When in public view, the mullah is mobile, always walking briskly with his eyes cast at his feet. It is said that a mullah should never be caught glancing at a woman.

I desperately desired to sit at the feet of these exotic preachers and to immerse myself into their world as best an American can. But there were obstacles and dangers. As recent as 1963, the mullahs had led an uprising against the government over certain matters. One grievance was the government's granting women the right to vote. Another was the privilege extended to American military and diplomatic personnel of diplomatic immunity. It was said that several thousand people lost their lives in battles in Tehran and Qum.

I discovered that I had two advantages in preparing the way to meet mullahs. Student friends who were practicing Muslims were more than happy to acquaint their professor with their preacher, and I loved tea. I had been raised in a family that drank ice tea, even drinking it at summertime breakfasts. But in Iran there was a difference. Tea was served hot and strong. For sugar there was a cube which you placed between your teeth and sipped the hot tea to melt it. I do believe, however, if I had not been a professor of anthropology, I would not have had the entré into the mullah's turf.

Mrs. Teherani, a young student of mine who was married to an architect, arranged a meeting between her mullah and me. I had noticed every day she wore a black scarf, dress, and stockings to classes. She informed me that her father had died the early part of the year, and it was the Iranian custom to wear black for one year after the death of a close relative. I learned that the mullah of her village mosque, who had buried her father, had moved to Tehran and that she frequently visited him and his family. When I showed interest in meeting him, she arranged a time in his home.

Mullah Abbas's house peeked over a high wall along a narrow alleyway deep in south Tehran. The southern part of the city houses the less affluent. Since there are fewer parks in this area, the children play in the streets. As we approached the rusted iron gates to gain entry into the courtyard of the house, the kids stopped their play to gaze at me—an utter foreigner to them. Leaving our shoes at the door of the house, we were led by a young boy to an upstairs room. It was empty except for a huge, brilliant carpet that covered the sizable floor and some cushions used for backrests which leaned against the walls.

Mrs. Teherani sat on a cushion to one side of the room, covered in her chador (veil). I sat to the other side, wondering if I should place my legs in the Yogi stance, the knee-bend position, or just let them naturally flop. A young son served us steaming hot tea as we awaited the appearance of the mullah. As I fiddled with the carpet, I noticed another carpet of near equal beauty beneath it. Many Iranians have their bank accounts on the floor.

A feigned cough from the hallway interrupted our tea drinking, and in a few seconds a median-sized man entered the room robed in a black cloak which flowed to the carpet. A black turban upon his head matched his thick black beard, and he held in his hands a string of one hundred small agates. Mullah Abbas warmly greeted Mrs. Teherani and me, shaking my hand which surprised me, and ordered for more tea to be served to us. He then took his seat on a well-worn cushion on the opposite side of the room.

By the fourth cup of tea, the mullah and I had warmed up to conversation beyond the weather, my health, my family's health, and the taxi ride. In fact, he had come over to my side of the room and removed his black turban. When a mullah wears a black turban, as opposed to a white one, it signifies that he is a descendant of the prophet Mohammed, and more people will honor him for his lineage.

I was surprised by the easiness with which he spoke to me. "I used to be the preacher in Mrs. Teherani's village until I was forced to leave. How I loved the small village life, its simplicity, its cleanliness, its purity. And people, especially young people, would come to the mosque for prayers and festivities. It was Allah's most favored place." I debated in my mind if I should pursue the reason why he was forced to leave the village and decided to wait, if not to let it go entirely.

He continued, "Tehran is too large a city. It is dirty and corrupt. There are more cinemas than mosques to claim people's attention. Islam is not strong in the city. In the village my wife and I were respected. I was sought out for counsel by the people. My house was full all the time. Now, my sons and I do the shopping in the streets and my wife stays at home."

I quizzed him about the new religious corps which the government was preparing and sending out to the villages to teach Islam to the people. I realized I had hit upon a sore spot.

Mullah Abbas ordered more tea for us and encouraged Mrs. Teherani to visit with his wife in an adjoining room. He, his eldest son, and I formed a circle around our cups of tea and sugar cubes. Mullah Abbas fingered nervously with his prayer beads and said, "These young men are good Shiites when the government conscripts them for service in the religious corps. But they are corrupted. And they are sent to the villages to teach modern political doctrines. They cause friction between the mullahs and the mosques. Their eyes fall upon the women. They are a failure at their work. Most of them leave after several months. This is the problem with government interference into religion. When I was in the village, people in marital difficulty could come to me and receive a true and speedy answer to their problem at no cost. Now they must go to the government court and hire a lawyer. For example, a man and woman separate over who shall pay for the baby's milk. By the time it is settled in court, the baby has grown up and married."

Mullah Abbas' eldest son sat quietly, and the few times he attempted to enter the conversation, his father silenced him. At this point in my visit, the mullah was having two glasses of tea served to me at once and nervously counting his prayer beads. I knew that social amenities would expect me to continue to drink, but I also knew something about body chemistry and less about Persian toilets. It was really time to excuse myself, yet I had a burning wish to know why the mullah had left the village. And then it happened.

He eyed me eyeball-to-eyeball. "Mr. Professor! You are an intelligent man. You would make a good Muslim. You will not learn Islam from the university, but you can learn it from me and the books I can provide you. The authorities have prohibited me from preaching from the mambar in the mosque. If I preached from the mambar

I would say the things which are in my heart and head, and they would put me in prison. But you can come to my humble home and I will teach you all I know."

Since I was a scholar of Islam, I thanked him for his gracious invitation and in return invited him to visit in my home. As Mrs. Teherani and I departed the house and replaced our shoes, the eldest son asked if he might visit me. I thought silently that he had much to say outside the presence of his father and encouraged him to come. Mullah Abbas placed a book on the history of Shiism in my hands as I left, fully confident that I would read it.

During the taxi ride to our homes, Mrs. Teherani explained the predicament of Mullah Abbas. She said the mullah had become quite vocal in his preaching against the intrusions of the government into the affairs of the mosque in the village. When he continued against the warnings of the authorities, they forced him to move out of the village. I realized that I had quickly learned one thing. If you drink enough tea, the dam of knowledge is cracked to allow deep immersion into another's life. I made a promise to visit the mullah again to say a few things of my own.

A favorite place to drink tea is in the Tehran covered bazaar, the world's largest. I often traveled to the bazaar just to be a part of the endless parade of colorful humanity. Any of several teahouses provide a bird's eye view of human, animal, and cart traffic. The teahouse offers a simple table and chair for the Iranian pause that refreshes. It also sends out waiters with trays of cups of tea delicately balanced on their heads as they disburse them to shopkeepers in the winding, narrow alleyways deep in the bazaar.

I frequently met my favorite Muslim seminary student in the teahouse. For the price of a dime we could sip two cups of tea apiece and chat for hours oblivious to all the hustle about us. Hasan was a village boy who had journeyed to Tehran to find work. His father was a farmer who had encouraged his son to be a mullah. Of all the professions, his father respected the mullahs who represented to him the height of honesty, sanctity, and concern for the family of Allah. Hasan had often heard his father say, "My son, if you will become a mullah I know you will take care of your mother and me in our old age."

Hasan had studied religious subjects in the village school, but being often discouraged about his future prospects he set out to explore big city life. However, soon he discovered that all young men of a certain age were conscripted into the military forces. One way out for him was to become a mullah. After all, had not his elderly father desired it of him? So he abruptly quit his job in an engineering firm and enrolled in a seminary attached to a city mosque.

Hasan was thirty years old now, and he felt that he had very little to show for his life. Over those cups of tea he used to lament, "If I had worked at engineering, I would now possess a wife, a child, a home, a car, and a good life. But what do I have? A few books! A small room at the seminary with a bed and a table! A little food to warm on my charcoal fire! A turban and a robe which I wash once a week with my body! And a friend or two who drink tea with me in the bazaar!"

To be sure Hasan had his problems, but they were not all that bad. I used to visit him in his dormitory room at the seminary. A small four by six foot Persian carpet adorned the rough second floor room that overlooked the courtyard of the mosque. Two framed pictures hung over the well-worn cot. One was of the prophet Mohammed, holding the Qur'an in his hand. The other was of Ali with raised sword in his hand. By enrolling in the seminary, Hasan was given a modest stipend for the purchase of necessities—enough to create for him a bare existence. But he wanted more. And so did the other new breed of seminarians.

The students at the Faculty of Islamic Theology where I taught were developing into a new mullah type, but they were university trained students. The government was preparing these students to shed the garb of the mullah and don Western-styled clothing to teach in the elementary and secondary governmental schools. These students were more sophisticated in their backgrounds and lifestyles and often ridiculed those students who continued to wear the traditional turban and robe.

But Hasan's seminary was still very traditional. And yet it had to contend with the obvious and subtle pressures of changing values exerted upon it by the surrounding social forces. Did a mullah really have the chance of receiving the respect of a young generation as Hasan's father had innocently believed? Hasan had once told me of walking past two young girls without chadors (veils) in a street near the seminary. One of the girls said to him and his mullah friend, "Do you want to drink my milk?" which to any Persian male means "come and lie with me!" Often, Hasan seemed to be obsessed with the subject of sex, speaking of the infidelity between husbands and wives, women in miniskirts and without chadors, and the loose talk heard in the streets and on the public buses.

Several times when I called on Hasan at the seminary, his mullah friend, Ahmad, was there. Ahmad was a blind mullah who traveled to Tehran from his distant village to catch up on his studies. Ahmad had once made the pilgrimage to Mecca in anticipation that Allah would restore his sight because of his obedience. Hasan respected Ahmad and used to tell me, "Ahmad is a very religious man, for what blind man would continue to pray to Allah if Allah would not cure his blindness? He is the kind of man you could leave your wife and money with and he would respect both."

One day as Hasan and I drank tea and ate oranges and cucumbers in his room, a short, chubby mullah entered. Mullah Kareem, a longtime friend of Hasan, presided over the activities of a nearby mosque. He was a jocular man with whom one immediately felt comfortable. After exchanging greetings, he delivered some books to Hasan. Upon learning of my interest in Islam, he invited me to come to his mosque for noon prayers the next day. I readily accepted his offer.

I was so eager to attend the noon prayers on time that I arrived in front of the mosque twenty minutes before noon. The mosque was a newly constructed one, quite simple with no minaret. Adjacent to it was a well manicured park with grass, shrubbery, walkways, and a small pool. The doors to the mosque were locked, but as if my presence was expected, the servant came from out of nowhere, warmly greeted me, and unlocked the doors. He led me over to the only chair in the mosque and seated me beside the heated kerosene burning stove. Of course, I had removed my shoes at the entrance.

There I was. Alone! A foreigner! In the corner of a mosque! Waiting! A ten step mambar stood in one corner, decorated in a green silk material and calligraphied in Qur'anic sayings. A huge, one-piece Persian carpet covered the floor. Qur'ans were scattered about the carpet, as well as pieces of clay from the holy city of Mecca on which the prayers would touch their foreheads as they knelt in prayer. A larger stove burned in the center of the room since cold weather had begun. On one wall a rack housed pajama-type clothing which would be used in the prayer rituals.

The silence within the mosque and my musings were interrupted by the entrance of the first Muslim From his appearance he was a street-sweeper. His tattered clothes, his worn cap, and the holes in his socks indicated he was a man of the streets. He glanced suspiciously over at me, nodded his head in recognition, and assumed a spot at the very front of the mosque. The second man to enter was a merchant from the bazaar, dressed in trousers and coat with an open shirt and a wide-brimmed hat. He conspicuously fingered his prayer beads as he sat on the carpet awaiting the mullah. Then, several clerical and bureaucratic types in suits and ties entered. Before they proceeded to the front of the mosque, they donned the pajama pants hanging on the racks so that their clothes would not be soiled and wrinkled.

After some thirty men had positioned themselves in rows on the carpet, Mullah Kareem entered the room, came over to my corner and greeted me, and then took his place before the rows of men. While small chitchat occurred, one of the men came to me and invited me to join them on the first row as their honored guest. He insisted that they would teach me how to pray. Completely caught by surprise, I muttered something in an unknown Persian tongue which he seemingly understood and which I can't recall. He smiled at me, told me to call the servant if I needed anything, and returned to his place before the mullah.

Mullah Kareem faced the men as they all sat in Yogi style upon the carpet. He introduced me to them as the honored friend of Hasan, as a noted professor, and as a good man. He then admonished them to be faithful in their prayers whether at his mosque or a mosque in their neighborhood. Then a man in a black Fez ascended to the third step of the mambar and chanted a portion of the Qur'an for about five minutes. At various intervals the men would repeat the name of Allah in unison. Mullah Kareem turned to face the mihrab, which indicated the direction of Mecca, and began to lead the men in their prayers. In complete imitation of the mullah, the men knelt, bowed their foreheads on the clay pieces, and stood erect, all the while repeating various expressions of Mullah Kareem. After twenty minutes the prayers were completed, and the men gathered in small groups round the floor as the servant brought tea to them.

The servants had served me numerous cups of tea while the prayers were being said, and though I had hesitated to drink it, he insisted that it was proper. Mullah Kareem came to me and led me to the various groups around the carpet for further introductions. I was amazed at the seemingly ease with which these men of diversified backgrounds blended: the educated with the uneducated, the street-sweeper with the government bureaucrat. They all invited me to return to the mosque.

As Mullah Kareem and I left the mosque together, he related the tragic story of his six year old son's death three weeks earlier. He said that his wife had not stopped crying over the loss of her son. I expressed my sympathy to him and explained why I had not come down to the front row to participate in their prayers. I told him I was a praying man because I was a Christian. I told him that we Christians offered our prayers in the name of Jesus Christ who answered prayers both in times of happiness as well as sadness and suffering. I assured him that I would remember his family's needs just as the men in the mosque had remembered the needs of all their Muslim brothers and sisters. Mullah Kareem grabbed my hand tightly, profusely thanked me for my interest in his problems, and insisted that I return to the mosque soon. Later, when my wife was hospitalized with a serious surgical problem, Mullah Kareem telephoned to tell me he had prayed for my wife in the mosque in the name of Jesus Christ. Certainly, tea for two and more had developed in my encounters with the mullahs.

The mosque of Mullah Kareem was small in comparison with the Husain Mosque near my home. I frequently passed by its doors at whose steps blind beggers lay and wondered what it was like inside the mosque and courtyard. The Persian fairy who ushered me through the two iron gates of the mosque was a young male student interested in the precepts of Christianity. He contacted the mullah of the Mosque, explained to him of my interest in Islam and my professorship in the college, and soon Mullah Reza extended to me an invitation to visit him in his office.

The appointed night arrived, and a little anxiously I caught a taxi that took me to the mosque door. A chadored woman with begging cup in hand edged up to me as I approached the door and promised to pray for me in the name of Allah if I would only give her bread money. I stepped over the still form of a sleeping derelict and entered the courtyard. Evening prayers were concluded, and the only noise in the courtyard came from the splash of the water fountain into the surrounding waters of the pool. An hour earlier I could envision hundreds of Muslims washing their faces, arms, elbows, and feet in preparation of purification for prayer.

A servant greeted me with the words, "Mr. Professor! Welcome! Please follow me." He led me to the second floor office of Mullah Reza, and as I entered the spacious room, the mullah greeted me warmly. He was a heavyset man with pronounced wrinkles upon his forehead and a rather full white beard. He wore a richly tailored black robe and a starched white turban. I could quickly see that he was a bishop type. He informed me that a board of trustees' meeting was just concluding, and introduced me to the various men around the room. I was given the seat of honor on the sofa nearest to the table full of Lebanese apples and oranges, Iranian cucumbers, pistachios, and candies, and American brand cigarettes. Iranians always preferred to impress their guests with foreign brand cigarettes, and most mullahs smoked.

Amidst tea drinking and eating, we rapidly became acquainted. One of the trustees was a principal of a high school. Another was a retired bazaar merchant. Two of the men were rather affluent landlords and landowners. After we had eaten and chatted for some time, Mullah Reza suggested that all of them give me a tour of the mosque facilities. It reminded me of a Southern Baptist church complex. The office in which we met housed the business and financial records. Off to its side was the private study and library of Mullah Reza. The study contained a carpet and a small desk which rose about twelve inches off the floor. The mullah told me he sat on the carpet and read from the Qur'an placed on the desk. His library contained volumes in six different languages.

The ground floor of the same building housed a library and lecture rooms. We crossed the courtyard and entered the mosque proper. A twelve step mambar adorned one corner of the huge hall, with intricate hand-cut designs in its polished wood. Several chandeliers hung from the ceiling, glistening with crystals. The floor was layered with several carpets. Mullah Reza especially pointed out the sunken mihrab in the floor at the front of the mosque which was his spot to lead the people in their prayers. He noted that it was lower than the main floor to symbolize the humility of the mullah who presided over the prayers. Tall curtains to the rear separated the place of the women worshipers from the men.

In the foyer between the mosque and the main lecture hall was a huge shoe rack where worshipers placed their shoes before entering the mosque. As we entered the salon, or what I labeled the auditorium, one of the trustees spoke up. "I gave the monies for this salon so it could be built to educate our people in the true values of Islam. Every Friday evening we have special lectures here and it is filled to capacity." I estimated that some six hundred people could be seated. The room was constructed similarly to a Protestant church. A raised platform contained a podium and chairs. Sophisticated audio equipment carried the lectures into other classrooms and into the courtyard. A gradually rising elevated floor contained rows of cushioned seating. Four chandeliers graced the ceiling.

Mullah Reza spoke up. "Professor Braswell, you will have to come to some of our lectures on Friday evenings and hear some of the most noted and inspiring speakers on Islam in our country. You know that in a week's time there may be two thousand people frequenting our mosque." The hour was late, and the men had been at the mosque for meetings prior to my coming. I decided to strike while the iron was hot, so I invited the mullah and his board to my home for an evening of discussion. They unanimously consented—to my shocked mind, and we departed with amiable farewells.

I was elated when I arrived home to tell Joan of our soon to be guests. What would we serve them? Better yet, who would serve them, Joan or myself? Since Joan did not wear the chador, would it be offensive to the mullah and the other men if she were present? It all seemed so unreal to have a mullah and his board visiting in our home.

The evening arrived to entertain our guests. Joan had decided to be present with me to greet them at the door. Then she would remain in the kitchen to prepare the tea, pastries, and fruits, and at the proper time pass them through the serving window for me to serve. In this manner she would not be conspicuous. Sharply at eight the bell rang and the entourage of four entered our home. Again I was surprised that the mullah shook Joan's hand, for I had heard repeatedly that a strict Muslim practitioner would not touch a woman other than his wife.

The men seemed friendly enough in our initial conversations. But soon I began to feel a seriousness to their questions. Mullah Reza quizzically commented, "Why does America support Israel against the Arabs? How can two million people in Israel be as important as one-hundred million Arabs? Only this morning in the newspaper I read where six million Jews in your country out of two-hundred million population control the press and television. Where is the American help for the Arabs? There was also a picture in the paper of naked slaves in South Africa working in the gold mines in which the Church of England had shares. Professor Braswell, do you know that we Muslims pray every day in our mosques for our Arab Muslim brothers to be liberated from their oppression?"

Mullah Reza had never intended for this matter to be a subject of our conversations. He only desired to score points and then move on to the matters of which he thought I was most interested. "Professor, are you Roman Catholic or Protestant?" I replied, "Protestant." He continued, "Does not the word, protestant, mean you protest against the things Allah abhors?" I readily agreed that the ideal for Christians was to act affirmatively in the teachings and ministry given to them by Jesus Christ. "In our mosques everyone knows he is welcome to come to prayers, to listen to sermons and lectures, and to be with his brothers and sisters. There are no classes of people according to Islam. If the Shah or a beggar comes to prayers, they are both treated equally. A Muslim is really a brother to each other Muslim, is equal to each other, is pure and clean in his practice of Islam, and if there is any inequality, it is because of the knowledge of Islam one possesses."

The trustee who was a high school principal had been fidgeting with his prayer beads while the mullah expounded upon Islam. Then he spoke. "I think the learned Professor ought to know of some of our difficulties in Islam as well as some of our good works. There is conflict in our religion between various authorities. Mullah Reza attempts to speak in the name of the prophet and the Imams. Others in our country attempt to speak in the name of political expediency. Some of our religious leaders are now in political prisons because they have spoken the true precepts of Islam. Many of our religious leaders are muzzled like dogs. They want to bark but cannot, because they will be persecuted or destroyed. Our religion does not promote corruption and the pillage of people as we now see in the land. We, too, desire to be protesters in the call to return to true Islam, but the times are very difficult for that."

In their presence, now, I was both scholar and Christian, but I also remembered that I was host. Joan's plan was put into action. I went to the serving window, and from that vantage point, carried all the refreshments to the men for their enjoyment. Drinking and eating seemed to turn our discussions to lighter subjects. We compared the architecture of the mosque with the church, agreeing that both were beautiful in their own individual ways. Mullah Reza described his own theological education and asked me to do the same. One of the men asked me to describe the differences between Tehran and Washington, D.C. And so the evening passed.

As the men departed, the mullah invited me to come to a Friday lecture to be their honored guest. I consented to go the next week, and they expressed delight. They reminded me to thank my wife in their behalf for the delicious refreshments, and they were off down our narrow alleyway.

The evening had been well spent. It was not every day that a mullah and his board visited a foreigner's house. Why had they come? Much, much earlier I had read E. A. Bayne's book in which he commented on several conversations he had with the present Shah. He related one incident in which a young scholar had visited in the homes of some mullahs in a village in Iran and the next morning found himself in the local police station being interrogated. When Bayne asked the Shah's opinion, the Shah stated that it was only natural for the police to be concerned over a foreigner visiting in the homes of mullahs. And now mullahs were visiting in my home.

There had been some genuine exchange. I had attempted to be a good listener and not to press deeper into matters which were not rightfully in my domain. Yet, there seemed to be an eagerness on their part in the frank sharing of their concerns. What a wonderful magic the tea of Iran creates. At noon the next day, just before Mullah Reza led his people in their prayers, he telephoned me to reissue me the invitation to the lecture and said, "We want to hear more of your protesting." I guess I had made a beginning in the world of mullahs and mosques.

3 The Unveiling

Upon first glance into the streets, one might think of Iran as a man's world. Or in one's first visit to an Iranian home the male figures might seem to predominate. But it is really not so. The Persian woman is a powerful one and portrays a mystique of her own. She is beautiful in her own right, a lord over her household, a manipulator of her men, a gossiper on every social occasion, an envier of other women more beautiful and richer than she, and a thorn in the flesh of those who would attempt to usurp her carefully guarded role in society.

And yet, in modern day Iran, there is such a contrast among the women. Reza Shah in the decades of the twenties and thirties attempted to force modernization upon his people, including a fiat commanding women to shed the chador and to dress in Western-styled clothes. Women were encouraged to attend the colleges and universities springing up in Iran and to avail themselves of clerical work. Polygamy and divorce customs and laws were changed to favor the status of women in Iranian society. The present Shah's several consorts have been models of Westernization for the women.

On a normal day's stroll down a thoroughfare of Tehran, one may see women dressed in the traditional chador, covering themselves completely except for eyes and nose. Other women may hang the chador loosely over their heads, revealing bright Westernized clothing beneath the flowing outer garment. Many women, especially the students and young mothers, dress without use of the chador and may be seen in pants suits. On one occasion near the University of Tehran, I was present when a gust of wind lifted a chador above a young lady's head and revealed that she was wearing hot pants.

I happened to be teaching a graduate class in the Faculty of Islamic Theology of the University of Tehran when several Iranian female students were admitted. Several years prior to that time, the authorities had attempted to enroll women students, but a strong contingency of mullahs had protested so violently that the scheme was dropped. Later, the time had ripened and three women were enrolled in my class.

All three were beautiful, married, and intelligent. But they were an exclusive club. They always wore the chador to the campus and into the courtyard, but laid it aside in the classroom. The back row always seemed reserved for them. In fact, I believe the men consistently came early in order to get the front seats to keep the women in their place. In class discussions the ladies seldom spoke, either out of respect for the mullahs or fear. They often remained after class to discuss questions which they had about the lecture, usually under the scrutinizing eye of a male student. The girls scored quite well on their tests and often outshone the male students in their assimilation of knowledge. The following year more females were admitted to the school.

The women, however, always felt under extreme pressure to demonstrate to the authorities, to the male students, and to their families that they could excel in a man's world; in fact, a mullah's world of learning. Students often brought gifts to me just prior to or directly after the final examination. It was always an awkward situation for me. Should I accept a small lambskin, or a picture of Mohammed the prophet, or a finely made Persian miniature? How could I offend the cultural tradition? I learned to give enough tests to the class before the final days so that by the time of gift-giving the grading results were already obvious. Thank goodness they didn't begin giving gifts at the beginning of the term. The ladies usually invited me for a deliciously cooked meal at their homes.

One of the strangest incidents which happened in my class concerned a female student. The Iranian chador is used for a variety of purposes. Traditionally, it has been used to cover the female that her sexual attractiveness might not be exposed to the male. But I am told that the chador is a flop in this regard, for the male sees through it. If nothing else, it excites his imagination. The chador also serves to allow a woman to go out in public with little worry about dressing up. There are other practical uses for the chador, and I learned first hand about one of them.

Cheating on examinations has not been considered one of the worse moral disorders within Iranian society. Since my cultural traditions varied from those of my Iranian friends, I at times had to adjust my ways of examining. At one time I gave individual oral examinations to every one of my students in several classes. However, on one occasion I gave written exams. A strange thing happened. One of the ladies wore a chador to class and kept it tightly about her body. Never before had the ladies veiled themselves in the classroom, and especially, this young girl who had always clothed herself in the tightest and most revealing knit sweaters from the boutiques of Tehran.

What a scene! A mullah dressed in turban and robe humming a prayer to Allah for an added portion of knowledge! A young lady in blouse and skirt writing away her expertise on the paper before her! And this beautiful and sexy young lady all veiled, fidgeting beneath the chador for some hidden knowledge! Tens of others cast furtive glances at her, well aware of her "cheating" ways. I was not about to unveil her then and there. I was later to learn of her fear of failure and the fantasies of suicide which float through many young Iranian minds because of family and peer pressures to succeed.

Just as I had desired to fathom the heart of Islam by entering the mullah's world, so, too, I wanted to see what the religious turf of women was like. And what a rich and exciting turf it is! It is the ambition of every good Iranian Shiite Muslim to make the once in a lifetime holy pilgrimage to the city of Mecca in Saudi Arabia. It is mandated in the Qur'an if one is healthy and financially able. Although thousands of Iranians make the pilgrimage (hajj) to Mecca yearly, most people do not make the trip in their lifetime. So they employ substitutes. There are thousands of pilgrimage places in Iran to which the faithful go. These shrines have become through the years natural gathering places for women.

One of my students, Mrs. Ferideh Paymani, asked me one day if I would desire to visit a nearby shrine dedicated to a famous Muslim saint. I literally jumped at the opportunity and we planned to go the next afternoon. In my anticipation of visiting Islamic persons and places, as well as teaching in Muslim strongholds, I had earlier grown a beard. Mullahs look upon a beard as a status symbol of religiosity, while I looked upon my own growth as a means to shield my pale American face. I surmised that I was as ready as one could be in my condition to enter a Muslim shrine.

By taxi, Ferideh and I wound our way through pedestrians, bike pedalers and other taxis to arrive at the shrine entrance. I could already see that its premises were a beehive of activity. I invited Ferideh to have a cup of tea at a small teahouse across the street so that I might watch the flow of human traffic in and out of the shrine and talk to her about the women's pilgrimage to this place. Ferideh was a middle class, educated young lady who still practiced her religion, so I knew that she had firsthand experience about the shrine.

As we sipped tea, she in her chador and I in my dark suit, she told me about the shrine. "The pilgrimage is a social occasion, and the shrine has gained popularity throughout the ages because it brings people together. It is a leisurely day out on picnic for a nation that has not had much facility for public entertainment. I am certain that television, sports stadiums, youth centers, and public parks have reduced the numbers of the pilgrims in our time, but still many women come to these places."

I had noted as she talked that very few men were visible around the shrine, and I asked her why. "In Iran it is easy for men to have social meetings during their business and working hours in their shops, in the bazaar, in the mosques, and in the teahouses. But women have had difficulty in mixing with the outside world, and the shrine has been one place where they have had freedom to leave the home. Household business, though enjoyable at times, can become monotonous when repeated every hour of every day of every year. The housewife needs to get away from the house sometime and somehow. The pilgrimage is just the right thing since it gains merits from Allah for both the woman in her obedience and for the husband who allows his wife to go. Thus, the Iranian woman, wearing her new chador, hanging her bright jewelry around her neck, and applying her rose water perfume, sets off happily to challenge the wife of the goldsmith or the daughter of a cotton merchant as they worship and gossip in the courtyards of the shrine."

"But what about the saint?" I interposed. "Are these ladies religiously motivated to come to the shrine?"

Ferideh smiled and stirred a bit restlessly underneath the chador. She was not used to wearing the chador at home, or in class, or even in the public streets. But on this occasion every woman near the shrine was visible in her flowing veil. "If it were not for the saint," she laughingly said, "I would be unveiled." She then became serious. "The shrine visit is above all a religious occasion. In the inside of the main hall where the tomb of the saint is located no one talks or asks questions—that is loudly. A continuous whisper and murmuring is heard of the visitors who call upon the authority of the saint to act as their intermediator and persuade Allah to fulfill their wishes. At the same time they seek the forgiveness and mercy of Allah, who can come to their rescue and solve all their problems. Here, true faith is observed. Here, some meditation and deep thinking takes place which, even if lasting only ten minutes during the whole day of outing, is still worthwhile.

"Dr. Braswell, the pilgrims at times have reported miracles such as the healing of their relatives or themselves which proves to them the value of the shrine, the saint, and their faith."

As Ferideh talked, I had kept an eye on the happenings across the street. As the chadored women entered the gates of the shrine, it appeared that they had boxed lunches under their arms. I mischievously noted, "Ferideh, religion and pleasure can be partners."

This set her off on a bit of "women's lib." She braced herself and said, "I have already mentioned the monotonous nature of the Iranian wife's life. The Iranian woman has received an unfair amount of negligence and unkindness even in her own household. Her husband or the leader of her family has absorbed the major part of the family's attention. And her children have occupied the rest of it. This has left no room for her to receive any care. The wife has always anticipated the sad possibility of being replaced by a younger bride. She has seldom experienced any sense of security, and in order to challenge any forthcoming danger, she has had to rely upon her skills as a housewife.

"The only suitable occasion to show this skill has been in a Rowzeh Khane, a Sofreh, or a day's pilgrimage to the nearby shrine. The poor Iranian wife has had to identify herself with the tenderness of her Shamies (a kind of hamburger), with the appropriate taste of her Sholeh Zard (a kind of rice pudding), and with the delicacy of her Halvah (a kind of sweet), which she prepares for her guests on these occasions. When she goes on pilgrimage, she takes with her some skillfully roasted nuts flavored with salt and lemon juice and distributes them in the shrine and among the women. She prepares dates or Halvah Loghmehs (sandwiches). She identifies herself with the variety of sherbets that she can make in her house. In this way she enjoys the approval of her friends, her husband, and her in-laws, which at least causes some satisfaction in her empty world of desires.

"Dr. Braswell, you are right. We Iranian women do mix pleasure and religion. We make some gossip which is quite relaxing and at the same time quite releasing. For after all, how can an inferior in rank injure the superior if not by words of gossip and shame? The shrine is usually packed with women who gossip for hours. But the pilgrim also cries her heart out to the saint. She literally shakes the shrine as she expresses her sorrow and sings of her misfortune to the saint. Finally, she leaves the shrine convinced that the saint will not disappoint her and will answer her prayers and requests to him."

I had intently measured every word of Ferideh as she "lectured" me on the despair and aspirations of Iranian women. What a tea break this had been! It was now time to cross the street and take the plunge into the heart of the shrine. My anxiety was somewhat relieved since I had noticed several Iranian men entering the shrine complex, for I certainly did not relish being the only male in that place, especially among all those veiled women.

As we entered through the wide, swinging gates and into the courtyard, I immediately realized that there were several buildings. The shrine proper lay directly in front of us. To its sides were mosques with their minarets ascending to the heavens. Off of the mosques were various sized tomb rooms where faithful and affluent Shiites buried their beloved near their favorite saint. In the center of the courtyard, where we were standing was a huge circular pool with a flowing fountain which accommodated the worshiping pilgrims who washed their feet and faces in the purification waters. From the outsider's viewpoint all seemed hustle and bustle. But what was happening inside the shrine, in the tomb rooms, in the mosques, and in the small active groups seated around the courtyard with their tablecloths spread, their teapots (samovars) heated up, their mouths in constant motion from either eating, or in Ferideh's words, gossiping?

"Ferideh," I anxiously whispered, "do you think I should venture inside the shrine?" She quickly answered, "You stay close to me. If the tomb-keeper should question you, my tongue is quicker than his and yours. Do not bother to be worried."

The shrine entrance was engulfed with silver mirrored material, on both sides were situated the shoe-keeper and his shoe racks. Now, barefooted, we proceeded into the gate entrance which was heavily decorated with mirror or silver plates. The gates were made of beautiful inlaid work. The hallways of the shrine represented the best of all Iranian handicraft and art skills. The shrine itself was made of silver globes in the shape of a small room. Over the entrance each pilgrim gazed at the inscription and recited it as a permission request to enter the "holy of holies." It read, "In the name of the almighty Allah, And in the name of Mohammed, And in the name of Ali, And in the name of Fatemeh, And in the name of Hasan, And in the name of Husain, And in the name of the descendants of Ali and Fatemeh, I seek the permission of entering the shrine of Abdol Abbas."

Ferideh paused to murmur the request as I looked at the tomb, remembering the shoe-keeper's words of counsel as I tipped him ten rials (fifteen cents), "Whatever you request from the saint (Imam), you will receive it." The tomb itself was covered with a green embroidered cloth filled with Qur'anic sayings. An ancient and evidently prized Qur'an lay on the tomb. Gold-plated bars surrounded the tomb, and the empty chasm between the bars and the tomb contained a scattering of coins which the pilgrims tossed for added merit.

A line of people, mostly women, circumambulated the caged tomb, reaching out for the golden bars, grasping them, kissing them, throwing coins, crying out prayers to the saint, and leaving weeping. Some of the pilgrims had bought candles from the shoe-keeper who lighted them. They took the candles to the candleholders near the tomb, made their requests to the saint, and placed them to slowly burn while they approached the tomb. I circumambulated the tomb too, not in the same mood and style as the others, but realizing the intensity of the experience for those who were involved in the occasion.

In the side mosques a few men and many more women were praying. Others were gathered around a mullah to hear him chant various stories of the saints. Often, I would hear the mullah begin his narrative acknowledging gratitude and respect to Allah, for his last prophet Mohammed, for Ali, Hasan, Husein, and the Imams, and for Noah, Abraham, Moses, and Jesus. Then he would recite the accounts of the martyrdom of the Shiite saints. Women would cry briefly, thank the mullah, tip him a small sum, and depart to the courtyard.

The courtyard was filled with women's groups seated around a tablecloth spread on the tiled floor. Sure enough, Ferideh was right. The women had brought their finest food snacks to the shrine to show off to all who would see or eat. The ladies with their chadors loosely draped around their shoulders, exposing their jewelry and colorful clothing, and I might add, their figures, beckoned to us to have some sweets. Ferideh asked them why they had made the pilgrimage. Now Ferideh's question may seem too direct for outsiders. But Iranians are very forthright. Iranians, especially women, will not hesitate to ask you your rent, your salary, and the quality of love for your wife. The women replied to her, sharply and clearly, "Because we do not like to go to night clubs or cafeterias." As we strolled on, Ferideh observed, "Dr. Braswell, I am certain they would very much like to do just that."

The variety of concerns expressed to Ferideh were quite interesting as we crisscrossed the courtyard. In the normal Iranian fashion, she would strike up a conversation with a woman, and the woman would immediately relate her reason for attending the shrine. One lady explained that her husband was in the army, and since he was absent quite often, she visited the shrine because of her loneliness. She indicated that she only had to spread her cloth, place on it bread and yogurt, and soon there would be women sitting around the cloth to share the food and conversation. One woman described the healing of her body which she attributed to vows taken at the shrine. So she comes frequently to the shrine to say her thanks to the saint. A young girl, twenty years of age and married to a policeman, had become discouraged because after three years she had borne no child. Her doctor had given her no hope, so she had come to the saint to request a baby. Numerous women gathered a crowd, called over a mullah to recite a narrative, paid him a small fee, and basked in the conversations that followed.

After two hours in a predominantly woman's world, it was getting time to depart. I had become weary of the stares of the gate-keeper, the shoe-keeper, and the tomb-keeper. Frankly I was tired because I knew I was out of place. To be sure, it was an educational and eye-opening experience. I had to be present to see this kind of unveiling. And I had questions. If Iranian men were so uptight about their women why did they allow them the day's outing? Could they think there is safety on religious turf? I had read and often heard that temporary marriages are easily obtained around shrine precincts. I was surprised at the casualness with which the ladies handled their chadors in the presence of the men in the shrine complex. The strange mixture of serious devotion and light-hearted bantering was intriguing to behold.

Ferideh, too, agreed that the visit must end, so we headed for the gate leaving behind the sounds of chanting, laughter, and feminine cries. Once inside the taxi, Ferideh quizzed, "Well, Dr. Braswell, what do you think of the shrine?" With a twinkle in my eye I replied, "I believe it is a place for women's liberation."

There was no way for me to know the class lines of the women at the shrine. I suspect they represented the spectrum of the affluent and the poor, the educated and the illiterate. I do know that the shrine met a deep need within their social and religious life. Women flock to more places than just the shrine to fulfill these needs. Ferideh had mentioned the Rowzeh and the Sofreh. These are meetings, especially for women, which are held in the homes. The Rowzeh Khane, literally meaning a chanting at home, is hostessed by a lady during the times of the year when Shiites reflect most intensely the martyrdom of their saints. The woman will invite a mullah and women guests for the occasion. Mrs. Parvin Reza, a middle-aged student of mine, invited me to a Rowzeh Khane held in one of her family members' home.

Parvin's son chauffeured me in their personal car to the home of his relative where the Rowzeh Khane was to be held. He told me that he had never attended a Rowzeh and that in his family only his mother occasionally put on her chador to go to hear the mullah chant. "Modern Iran," he said, "looks to other matters than crying over the dead." He also indicated to me that the university which he was attending was on strike because the students were protesting police intervention within the university grounds.

Upon arrival at the house, Mrs. Parvin Reza greeted me and introduced me to her uncle and aunt who were hosting the occasion. I noticed several women seated in the living room in their chadors. I was ushered into the adjoining room where the men were to sit. Within an hour's time, by 6 P.M., some thirty women, all veiled, had taken their places in the living room. There were to be three mullahs to chant the narratives of the saints for the audience. The first mullah arrived early, and was seated next to me in the room designated for the men. Before the mullah arrived, two of the host's daughters, beautiful teen-age girls dressed in black pants suits with their black finely combed hair flowing to their waists, served us tea, sweets, and Winston cigarettes. The girls donned their chadors in the presence of the mullah and kept them on until after the chanting was concluded. Several latecomers, forgetting to bring their chadors, stood at the door until the hostess fetched them emergency ones and then they entered the room.

Each mullah recited portions of the specific narratives for the day, and with each recitation the women cried, some more loudly than others. From my vantage point I could tell that all the furniture had been removed from the room, and cushions had been placed around the walls on which the women sat. A small stool had been provided for the mullahs. The eight men gathered in the adjoining room with me were merely spectators during the meeting. While the mullah chanted and the women cried, we men drank cup after cup of tea, talked and laughed, carried on business over the telephone in the room, and occasionally peeked toward the room of the women.

Mrs. Parvin Reza's father was present and informed me that this kind of meeting was an annual family affair. Each year, for five successive days, the family will employ three mullahs to come daily to one of the homes and lead the family members in commemoration of the saints' death. Since they invite a few neighbors and friends to the Rowzeh, the men and women are segregated. If it were solely a family affair, both men and women would sit together. "Why do they cry?" I asked him. Smoking his Winston, he replied, "The Iranian has deep feelings about his religion. You know the difference between the Sunni Arab Muslim and the Iranian Shiite Muslim. The Sunni Muslims killed one of our prominent saints and his family members, and since that day we have cried to Allah over that tragedy. Can you imagine killing a saint, his children, his brothers, wives, and cousins, all at once?" This was the only time I saw any of the men become emotional during the two hours I was there.

Remembering the directness of Ferideh in her questioning of the women at the shrine, I mustered up my courage and asked, "But why are you men not crying as the women?" Mr. Reza smiled, not offended at all by my question, and said, "This is really their meeting. Let them have their time of crying. We will have ours with the men in the mosque."

As the last mullah concluded his chanting and departed with the proper farewells to the men, the host jumped up from his chair and turned on the television just in time to get the evening news. As if the mullah's departure were a signal, the women dropped their chadors to the floor, opened up their packs of Winstons, and generated a noise that drowned out the voice of the new's commentator. It appeared that I was back in the same environment of the shrine.

Perhaps the heart of the religious world for Iranian women is the Sofreh, which literally means the spreading of a tablecloth from which food is either eaten or taken. The Sofreh is strictly a woman's world, and men do not show their presence. I can say one thing for my students in the various places I taught. They are intelligent, ingenious, and daring. One young lady came to me after class to relate that her aunt was giving a Sofreh. That was really not news for there are hundreds given over the city of Tehran daily. What was news was that she was inviting me to come and sit in a side room to observe the occasion. How could I refuse, unless I suspected that the women might see me, and in their emotional outburst around the tablecloth, perceive me as a Sunni and do me in. I decided to take the chance, and to complete the circuit of shrine, Rowzeh, and Sofreh.

The spreading of a tablecloth is a ritualistic occasion. The participants express both sorrow and joy as they hear narrations of the stories of the saints, and the women tell of the vows which have been granted to them by the saints. Sofrehs may be given for both large and small gatherings, depending on the affluence of the hostess and the importance of the vows. Often a female mullah may preside over the ceremonies.

My student and I arrived early at the home of Mrs. Azoudi, her aunt, for I had to be positioned in a location so as not to be conspicuous to the group of women and yet be able to observe the proceedings. Mrs. Azoudi was an aristocrat by the furnishings in her home, her demeanor, and her conversation. She had placed a curtain over a stairwell which would conceal me from the view of the group but which would afford me the privilege of observing the Sofreh. And the servant could walk up the stairs to serve me tea and refreshments at any time I desired. What more could I ask for?

Mrs. Azoudi's son had been involved in an automobile accident. She had vowed to Saint Abbas that if her son fully recovered, she would give a Sofreh in the saint's name. All the exquisite furniture had been removed from the living room. The fine Persian carpet, from wall to wall, served as seating, and a cloth was spread in the center of the carpet. The hostess had invited both family and friends. She told me that one must invite even the poorest women in order for the saint to be pleased. From my roost I observed the women as they entered, the rich and the poor. Some chadors were of fine silk and others were of plain cloth. Some deposited their Italian-and American-made shoes at the door, while others left behind their twenty rial (thirty cents) Iranian-made flip-flops. All gathered around the tablecloth, chatting, laughing and drinking their freshly brewed tea. In this jocular spirit where class lines seemed no bother, I wondered why I was discriminated against. But I drank my tea and ate my pastry, watching all the while.

By 5 P.M., sixty-two women had arrived and were seated around the cloth. A female mullah entered in her black chador streaming to the floor and took her designated place. For thirty minutes she narrated in chanting fashion the story of the saints, with particular reference given to Saint Abbas. She stressed Abbas' courage, loyalty, and perseverance. Some of the women wept. Then the mullah described a miracle which happened to one of her relatives through the power of Abbas. And she referred to the good heart of Mrs. Azoudi who trusted the saint and was rewarded in her faith. She counseled the women to obey all the rules of Islam. Then she offered prayers for the participants in the Sofreh, for their families, for those in hospitals, and for those in prisons.

At 6 P.M., servants brought in a meal of Ash Reste, Pilou lentil, nuts, fruits, and cake. I learned that women take no backseat to men in the enjoyment of the palate. In fact, around that tablecloth women reached, grabbed, and devoured like as on no other occasion I had witnessed. I must admit, it was good food, for the servant had brought the same kind up the stairs to me. At the conclusion of the meal, the mullah addressed the women on the subject of prayer. Then she digressed to the sins of lying, stealing, gossiping, and cursing. At one point, she asked for those who desired to make a vow to Abbas to light a candle. Several ladies followed her admonition. If their vows were granted, they, like Mrs. Azoudi, would be responsible for giving a Sofreh in honor of the saint. Her duties concluded, the mullah left the house. At the door I noticed that Mrs. Azoudi gave her an envelope which I assumed to be a gift of money.

Much small talk ensued around the tablecloth after the formal ceremonies were concluded by the mullah. One lady was rather loud in her storytelling. She had to be to gain the attention of the chattering ladies. She related that her doctor had told her she could bear no children. In desperation she had attended a Sofreh to honor Saint Abbas, and while there, had vowed to the saint to honor him the rest of her life if she could have a child. She was now a new mother, and all the women uttered "Ma'shalla" (Allah be praised) at her vow fulfillment in the name of Abbas.

By 8 P.M. the ladies began leaving. Mrs. Azoudi gave each one a bag of nuts (Agil), for it is believed that nuts taken and eaten from a Sofreh will bring good health to the participants and their families. Some of the younger women remained behind while the tablecloth was shaken over their heads to ensure they would be married before returning to the next Sofreh. Soon all the guests had departed, having cried over tragedy and loss as well as rejoicing over the health and happiness of the hostess and her son. After nearly four hours of concealment, and a foreigner's eye full of another part of a woman's world, I was ready to leave. I assured Mrs. Azoudi of my good feelings over the health of her son and over the good intentions of her heart. And I thanked her profusely for allowing me to observe the occasion. "Professor (Ostad), did you learn a lot?" she asked. I replied, "Because of your kindness I learned a lesson about the heart of your faith. And to tell you the truth, I didn't know there were female mullahs." And with a bag of nuts in my hand, and five other bags in my pocket, for Mrs. Azoudi had insisted that I take each of my family a bag for their good health, I caught a taxi home. Another unveiling! And I had escaped with my life.

Perhaps it is in the religious pilgrimages and rituals that most Iranian women feel their greatest sense of independence and freedom. For the most part fathers and husbands trust their daughters and wives in the sanctity of their religious turf, presided over by the women themselves. Yet, for many Iranian women the ambivalences of the female role in Iranian society are great. The king decreed that women discard the wearing of the veil. Yet, a woman on the city streets without the veil is game for the buttock-pinching of Iranian males. The Iranian man still thinks that a woman without the veil is provocative, displaying her loose morals before the public eye. He thinks he is accommodating her in her quest for attention. Especially, in the younger generation of youth, however, there is a new sense of identity and changing life-style.

In the past only males were educated in schools. Now females are not only encouraged but are required to attend school. In former times the sexes were segregated into different schools. At present, boys and girls attend the same classes. Often one will see a young girl leave her home wearing the chador. As she enters the grounds of the school, she will take it off, fold it neatly, and store it in her bag until she departs for home. She serves two worlds. She pleases her most conservative parents and observes the protocol of the predominant opinion of the street people, while at the same time she abides by the liberal policy of the government-run school of preparing its youth for the modern world.

Iranian women are deeply interested in their own unveiling. They have many models to follow, and there are many stimulants to their pursuit. Walking down the streets of Tehran, one may see on the cinema billboards glaring and raw examples of sex. The mullah was correct. There must be hundreds of cinemas in Tehran, and many seem to show westernized R and X rated movies. Often, I have seen long lines of both men and women awaiting the purchase of tickets, some women in chadors and some in thigh length skirts and tight blouses. Discotheques buzz with the Western beat of music and couples in dark corners. Iran has recently had a woman for minister of education. The king has designated his queen to reign until the crown prince comes of age if something should happen to himself. Women police officers patrol the streets, direct traffic, issue parking tickets, and ride motorcycles. Young ladies are recruited into the armed services. Divorce laws have been changed to protect and favor women from the whims of males.

A conspicuous place where the modernizing role of women is being prepared is Damavand College where I served on the faculty. Some six hundred ladies attend the four-year school which developed out of a former Presbyterian mission high school. It is presently operated by a board of trustees who are predominantly Iranian. The king has been a vital patron of the college. Besides receiving a liberal arts education, the women may concentrate on clerical courses such as typing and shorthand. The students are representative of middle class society with some ladies from the upper elites and some on scholarships from the lower classes. The student body still gives a blend of the ambivalences of the female in Iranian society.

Some of the more socially and religiously conservative students will wear a head scarf in place of the chador while they are on the campus. They will bristle and lament over the remarks of their more liberal fellow students that religion and Scriptures are guides for the illiterate. Some of the students from the upper middle class freely admit that they are bored at home and only get in the way of the servants at work. For them boredom is overcome five days a week with eternal gossip circles in the classrooms and in the courtyard on campus, with minor irritations of class attendance and assignments. Some are in the throes of marital difficulties and divorce proceedings. Others are caught between the generation gaps of parental values and new life-styles. A smaller number of the younger girls desire to excel in their studies in order to gain meaningful skills and employment both in Iranian business enterprises as well as in the hundreds of foreign companies established in Iran.

The irony of the woman's plight in Iran might be seen in the case of Ferideh. She was a beautiful woman, married, and possessed with a sense of a new destiny for the Iranian woman. Her parents were serious practitioners of their Muslim faith, and she had been reared in the same faithful observances. Her parents had directed her to the young man she had married. Her family was wealthy, and her husband's family was wealthy. One day over tea she leveled with me.

"A new day is coming for Iranian women. I not only feel it will happen, but I am experiencing it now. No longer will parents dictate who their daughter will marry. No longer will husbands expect their wives to spend all day prettying up for their return in the evening. No longer will women tolerate servitude in the streets and in the bazaar."

I had known Ferideh long enough to know she was an intelligent young lady, full of creativity and ambition. I also knew she lived in the special tension through which a society struggles when old social patterns are being replaced by the new and often frightful ways.

"But Ferideh," I interjected, "isn't your generation called upon to bear the sting of the change? Won't you really have to live with the old and the new?"

"Dr. Braswell, the books I have read at the college have opened up a new world to me. Right now, I fantasize about my future. I share my ideas with the others on campus, yet my family cannot understand. The most dangerous thing in Iran is for a woman to think for herself. The Iranian woman is a powerful person in the home when she directs the activities of the home, her children, her servants. She really is more powerful than her husband in the home. If you don't believe me, marry an Iranian woman. That is her hidden role. But in her public role she is restricted to a position of weakness. I believe the women you saw at the shrine are seeking a secure feeling and place in the world just as much as the girls at the college. The role of the woman in hidden places of importance and power has always been with us. The new day demands that we shed our veils and claim our places not only in the home but in the streets and in the work of our society."

I knew that Ferideh was not just speaking rhetoric. I agreed with her. In observing the shrine activities and the Rowzeh Khane and Sofreh, I had come to the conclusion that women were voicing more than a prayer to a saint for good health. They desired more for themselves. They prayed to escape the prisons of their souls. The shrine and the college were similar in one respect. They served as territories of escape for the day. I had already witnessed much unveiling, and more was sure to come. In another place and time in Tehran, a chic young lady out of desperation had offered her body in exchange for an educational reward. And Iranian women in their search for life had heard or read that in the Prophet of the Christian religion she might be free indeed. But in most places the unveiling was gradually occurring amidst laughter and mourning.

4 A Young Man Beats His Drum

Story telling is a favorite pastime in many of the teahouses across Iran. Iranian men will sit for hours, sipping tea or smoking the bubbling pipe, and listen to their comrades recite the lines of their famous poets, Hafez and Saadi. To me, one of the most fascinating adventures of an expatriate living in a distant land is to hear and see the life history of a native son. Hearing the stories makes the country real, and the people come alive. Of course, one individual does not make a country, and what he tells you and what you see must be weighed against every stitch and weave of the mosaic called the Persians. Surely there will be exaggeration, and at times a larger than life portrait. But the story he tells is worth listening to, as you trail after it in teahouses, alleyways, Chelo Kebab restaurants, pizza parlors, double-deck buses, taxicabs, and in the quietude of the home.

Cyrus is a young man in his twenties, handsome in face and figure, and fluent in three languages: Persian (Farsi), English, and the dialect of his native village. When I met him, he was preparing to come to the United States for his college education. But that is ahead of the story. He was born in a small town in northern Iran, the oldest of four children. His brother was two years younger and his sisters were thirteen and sixteen years younger than he. His early years were spent in a one-room, sparsely furnished house. At the age of four his mother taught him to read, write, and count. At age five his father bought him a first grade reader, and his mother taught him to read it. "When neighbors visited my home, my parents would have me recite the whole book, and everybody would praise me."

When Cyrus was in elementary school, his uncle on his mother's side taught him. Those early school years were unpleasant for him. Both his mother and uncle pressured him to be the first student in the class. He rebelled against the nagging, and he failed the fourth class. He blamed that failure on the constant pressures of his mother and uncle. "Many of my friends dropped out of school about this time to become apprentices to their fathers. It was a normal thing to do. But somehow I was abnormal and continued my schooling."

In these early years he was subject to many beatings from his mother. "My mother wanted me to be very organized. If my shoes and trousers were excessively dirty I was beaten, sometimes by her hands and sometimes with a stick. Once I took ten rials (fifteen cents) from the shelf to buy a small toy. My mother told my father about it and he beat me with a belt. The seed was sown in my heart to escape from home. I felt things deeply in my heart in those days. One night I remember my mother coming to my room after she had punished me. She thought I was asleep and leaned over and kissed me and said, 'Why do you make me hit you?' I used to think how strange that was. She beat me and at the same time loved me."

Cyrus used to go to the mosques with his boyhood friends, especially during the holy seasons. He liked the passion play of Saint Husain and remembered how some men cut themselves and let the blood run over the white robes they were wearing. At the end of the religious parades through the streets they would gather at the mosque for a large meal provided by a wealthy merchant. Cyrus recalls that his father reprimanded him for marching in these parades and characterized religion as nonsense and for the ignorant. He never attended the mosque with his father or mother, for his father would not go and his mother went with other women.

Cyrus' father was an industrious man. He had been cheated out of the family inheritance by his brother and had been left quite poor. Until Cyrus was twelve years old his father worked as an apprentice for a hatmaker in the bazaar. By saving a little money, he bought the appropriate tools to make hats. In the evenings he would make hats at home to sell to merchants in the bazaar. From the money saved from this extra work, he bought a shop in the bazaar and began making his special design of hats. It was about this time that Cyrus decided to run away from home. A friend and he caught a bus to Tehran, but word filtered through the various police checkpoints along the route. They were stopped and returned to their parents. The relationship between Cyrus and his parents changed at this juncture in his life.

"I think that my mother and father had learned a lesson from punishing me. It did them and me no good. I think that my father realized that I was becoming somewhat of a freethinker like he was. From the seventh to the ninth grades I became more independent. I would stay out late at night, even coming in after my father had arrived home from the bazaar, and they would not punish me."

But Cyrus' freethinking was to lead him into serious repercussions with his parents. An American Christian mission had come to his town, and he had begun to go to their meetings. "English was my favorite pastime both in school and whenever I could find an English-speaking foreigner in our town. The language came natural to me. I began going to the homes of missionaries and exchanging my Persian for their English. I am sure I learned more English than they did Persian. I learned to read the Bible in English, to pray, and to sing; all in a short time. And these people loved me."

But Cyrus was having more difficulties at home centering on the religiosity of his mother and the agnosticism of his father. His mother could not tolerate his courting of Christian missionaries, for after all, she was a staunch Muslim. And his father feared for his reputation in the bazaar. Cyrus recalled the arguments between his parents late at night as he listened to them from his bedroom. His father would accuse his mother for her lack of responsibility for raising him, and she would accuse the father for Cyrus' ill-behavior. "This was the first time my father ever seriously talked with me. You know what I mean, man to man. He reminded me that his grandfather was an important mullah who had been granted concessions by Reza Shah and had been held highly by the people in that province. He also told me that the bazaar merchants were complaining to him about my behavior because I was becoming too closely associated with the Americans. In the bazaar of a small town if one is not a Muslim, it is difficult to be accepted by the other merchants. And the people will not buy your products. My father did not practice any religion, but he pretended to be a good Muslim once he set up his business in the bazaar. Now he was afraid that I would cause real problems for him."

Cyrus realized the difficulties that both he and his family faced if his relationships continued with the missionaries. So he made his choice. He sought baptism in the church and the church sent him to Tehran for a summer conference. His decision to become a Christian and a church member was basically a decision to leave home and begin a new adventure. "I felt religious at the time. I knew for a fact that a group of people loved me and cared for me. And I feared that I would cause trouble for my family. I could not turn my back on a new world which opened up to me. I just had to go to Tehran."

His departure to Tehran marked the beginning of a new life for him. During the next three years he lived with various missionary families and taught Persian to them and to other foreigners. He finished his high school work by attending evening classes. "A boy of my age at this time of life would be under the control of his parents, would attend the mosque, and would be completely dependent upon his father for finances. But I was on my own, except for my friends the missionaries. I was able to earn enough money from my teaching to provide for my needs. My Christian friends gave me room and board, so I had no problem about money. I did have a problem about my religion. I was introduced to Christianity by a Presbyterian missionary, but by the time I made the rounds in Tehran, I had taught and lived with Independent Baptists, Pentecostals, Anglicans, and Seventh Day Adventists. I had been told not to smoke, drink, dance, or date by many of my Christian friends. I guess I became very confused."

Cyrus had been a good student in English since the ninth class and hungrily read any English books he could find. So finding a job teaching English was no problem. At that time Tehran was in the boom years with American businesses locating there and requiring all kinds of Iranian clerical and managerial help. There was a madness in the city for learning English in order to qualify for lucrative employment. In fact, Cyrus had more jobs than he could rightly fulfill for he was an excellent teacher. He taught English in high schools, in private institutes, in homes. He served as an interpreter at several foreign embassies.

"I was absolutely on my own after I finished high school in Tehran. Although I saw my Christian friends and went to church, I was not dependent upon them as before. I was making enough money to rent a small apartment and to buy some of the things I had desired as a small boy. At times I guess I really looked foolish to my neighbors. I bought a car and hired it out as a taxi during the day. You could do this in Tehran then and make good money. My friend drove it while I worked and we both made something out of it. I had always wanted a bicycle, but my father had been unable to buy me one. So I bought a bike, dressed up in my best clothes, and rode it through the streets. Then I would park it alongside my car. People thought I was mad. I was only trying to make up for the things I missed as a boy."

Cyrus admitted that he was a little wild. A former girl friend who had finished high school in his town came to Tehran to begin training in a nursing school. Cyrus posed as her brother to the landlord so she could stay in his apartment. Later, her two sisters moved in with them when they began their schooling in Tehran. Cyrus remembered those days as partying times. Since elementary school he had wanted a set of drums. He had always been musically inclined. He bought a set, learned to play them quite well, and he and the girls held dancing parties of their own. The old gang broke up when two of the girls married and the girl friend returned home.

"Occasionally during these years after high school I returned home. My parents were always happy to see me. You know how Iranians make such a fuss over long absences. There were always tears. My mother could never get over the fact that I had become a Christian. She still thought it was impossible, but I never argued with her. I did disagree with her over one matter. She tried to arrange a marriage between my cousin and me. My mother and her parents both pressured me, but I would not give in. My father hated her father because he was an alcoholic, so he was on my side. I don't know how many times my mother prayed in the mosque that the wedding might take place. I really think she thought that I would remain a Muslim if I married into the family."

Cyrus' brother had finished high school and was working with his father in the hat shop in the bazaar. He hoped to take the university entrance exams. His father had encouraged his two sisters to wear Western-styled dress and to go without the veil except in the bazaar. They were not allowed to see any young men. But his father seemed to be more relaxed around him.

"In my father's early manhood he had been attracted to the revolutionary spirit and had closely identified with our neighbor to the north. In fact, at one point in his life he had been imprisoned. When I visited home he related to me from his own independent spirit and free thinking. Often, I sensed a longing in his conversations to be a young man again. My father strongly counseled me to remain silent about politics. He said there would only be trouble for those who expressed their opinions."

From his first contact with Americans in his town, Cyrus had nurtured the ambition to go to America to study. He began to dream night and day of ways he might launch a magic carpet to what he considered the land of promise. It was at this point in his life that I met him. He was a mature young man, possessing a keen intellect and a pleasant disposition. A striking thing about Cyrus was that he smiled more than he frowned. When I asked him why more Iranians didn't smile on the streets, he said, "Their religion is really too heavy for them and their burdens of life constantly demand their attention. I smile because I am basically happy. My Christian faith, I guess, rests more on love than on law. For the Muslim it is exactly the reverse."

I became deeply interested in this young man who could sound a drum with different beats. He was a gentleman, a scholar, and a young, sensitive Christian. It seemed a great waste to Iranian soil if this young man were lost to it. This often occurs when a youth goes to America to study. He tastes the fruits of success, marries an American, and settles down in his adopted country. This is what the developing countries know as the "brain drain." I agreed to aid Cyrus in gaining some financial assistance to an American college, realizing his potential was great and hoping he would be able to make an abiding contribution to his native soil.

But Cyrus encountered two problems. Iran requires military service of all its youth. Before he could obtain an American visa he had to gain an exit permit from the Iranian government. An exit permit would only be granted him if he had completed the two years of military service. Cyrus had vowed he would escape the service just as he had fled his home and there was a way. In Iran there is always a way. Cyrus recalled that he had taught English to a famous woman artist who might help him in his predicament. "She is a lady who has influence in high places," he said. "In Iran all things are difficult, but some ways are made less difficult by power and money."

His woman friend did have a way. She knew a medical doctor who held the rank of general in the army and telephoned him about the plight of Cyrus. Cyrus' basic plight was his distaste for the military and his desire for exemption. The doctor agreed to examine him, and after a "thorough examination," according to Cyrus, his eyes were found too weak to qualify him for active service. Here was a scholar who could see into the mind of Shakespeare and could see the shores of America, but could not see his way into the gates of the military garrison. His "poor sight" cost him his car, which he sold to pay off the general.

Cyrus was not free yet. His second problem concerned a zero he received on a final composition paper in high school. Every graduating senior had to write a favorable essay on the "White Revolution." In 1963 the Shah of Iran had launched his peaceful revolution of land reform and better working conditions for both the peasants and the proletariats. It was called the white revolution in opposition to a red and bloody one. Every Iranian youth was taught the principles of the revolution. But more than that, every young person was indoctrinated to look perfectly upon the Shah and his revolution for the people. Under the guiding eyes of their teachers they were to hallow it in word and in deed.

"By the time I was a senior," Cyrus reflected, "I had read Shakespeare, Marx, Adam Smith, and Thomas Jefferson, as well as some of our best "underground" writers. I had adopted another religion, had left home, and had learned to be independent and free to a certain extent. I could not read without raising questions with the authors, and I could not write without being honest, not completely honest, but somewhat. So I wrote on my essay what I thought about the revolution, and it wasn't favorable. My teachers gave me a zero which meant that my transcript would be kept from me."

The particular college to which Cyrus was applying needed his transcript before considering his admission. To obtain the transcript meant that the zero had to be removed. Cyrus knew that this was a more difficult task than his exemption from military service, because there were more people to "see" in the educational bureaucracy. But he was not deterred. His gifts of language and money over a period of one year and worn-out shoes produced the needed transcript as well as a passport and visa. He was ready to go except for the farewells, and often they are deterrents.

In departing for the states Cyrus made a last visit to say goodbyes to his family. He said that his brother and sisters envied him in what they considered to be a chance in a lifetime. His father encouraged him to be loyal to himself and especially not to marry an American girl, for she could never be happy living in Iran. And his mother cried. "I was sad at the moment," he said, "and I would not be honest if I didn't say so. I was prepared to leave though, for I had really left home years before."

So Cyrus jetted off in the first plane ride of his life, loaded to the limit with what few valuables he had. I knew he would make a go of it. He had survived through all the turmoils of his early home life. He had mastered the mazeway of big city life, overcoming the tough obstacles of power and bureaucracy. He had a work scholarship at a stateside college which I had helped him attain. He was fluent in English and had a double portion of self-confidence. I suspected that he would follow his father's admonition to be loyal to himself, but I had my doubts about his advice on the American girl.

As Cyrus narrated his pilgrimage to me over a duration of time and in various places, it gave me the opportunity to critically look at the people among whom I lived and worked. When the parents are observed as experienced by Cyrus' story, several patterns are seen. The mother is a traditional, practicing Muslim who says her prayers, attends the mosque, and attempts to train her son in the observances of Islam. She is displeased with her son's change of faith and tries to woo him back with a planned marriage. The father presents quite a contrast with the patterns of the mother. He is not a practicing Muslim except when he uses the name to save face in the bazaar. He doesn't encourage his children to pursue religious interests. His political ideology and activity caused his imprisonment in earlier years, and he counseled his son to remain inactive and silent over political matters. He encouraged his son to follow his own interests and did not insist on a career for Cyrus in the bazaar as many Iranian fathers do.

Modern Iranian writers point out the changing ways of families as generation gaps occur. One writer says that the interrelations within the traditional family are based on the authority of the father and respect for his arbitrary decisions, as well as the mother's devotion to the son. But something is happening to modern Iranian youth which challenges this pattern. One novelist in a recent book portrays a young man who constantly lives in tension with his parents. In one scene the young man runs across a disenchanted group in front of the parliament building and says to the leader, "You are rebelling against the impossible repressions of our religious and cultural traditions, the morbid mysticism, the holy superstitions, the autocracy of well-intentioned but ignorant parents and teachers; the foundations of our society are autocratic." One sociologist asserts that Iranians claim that the family is a secure place, but he observes that though it is a place of intimacy, duplicity abounds in the marriages of convenience, in attempts to exploit others, in mistrust among the members, and in indifference to family sentiment.

One must be careful to analyze what Iranian writers say about the changes in their society. However, Cyrus appears to model much of their conjecture. He did break out of the authority-submission relationship to his father, but his father appeared to prepare his son for this liberation from parental authority from events within his own past. His revolutionary and imprisonment activities exemplified a break with the traditional past. He may have desired more liberation for Cyrus. Cyrus was bright enough to read the interaction between his father and mother and sense the encouragement from his father not to be chained to family or friends but to seek out his own future.

Within the Iranian family and society there are orientations toward the insecurity of the individual and mistrust toward one another. Cyrus' father voices insecurity when he warns his son of the consequences of political involvement. He expresses the fear of losing his status in the bazaar because his son has become a Christian. The mother's constant punishment of her son may have arisen from the insecurity of her role as wife and mother when her husband and son empathized with her so little. The insecurity of Iranian society is evidenced in the total disallowance of criticism against the king and the "White Revolution."

Social scientists generally agree that in nonparticipatory social systems governed by a closed elite, reliance upon intrigue and coercion is widespread, and the diffusion of mendacity as an acceptable mode of self-defense against the mighty is prominent. I think Ferideh hinted at this behavior in our conversation at the shrine. The king of Iran in his autobiography decries the fact that Iranians lie at their convenience. The king recalls that the Qur'an ranks lying as a cardinal sin, and he sadly quotes from the poet Saadi, "Words which beguile thee, But thy heart make glad, Outvalue truth which makes thy temper sad." Iranians early develop the doctrine and practice of dissimulation which basically is "conceal thy god, thy destination and thy creed." This permits an Iranian to pretend to be what he wants to be, whatever best serves his self-defense.

Folklore is replete with aphorisms of personality characteristics of residents of various cities and villages showing the symptoms of mistrust and exploitation. For example, an Isfahani is a native of the city of Isfahan. Other Iranians will say of those natives, "Isfahan is a paradise full of luxuries were there no Isfahani in it." Or others will say of the residents of the towns of Kashan and Qum, "A dog of Kashan is better than the noble of Qum, although a dog is better than the native of Kashan." Another example of the way people look at town-dwellers who are from different towns than their own is described in the saying about the people of Tabriz. "From a Tabrizi thou will see naught but rascality, even this is best, that thou shouldest not see a Tabrizi." The Iranian, then, often sees human nature as manipulative and opportunistic. Others will cheat him for they are exploiters. An everyday expression is, "Since there are devils in the guise of men, one should not give one's hand into every hand."

Cyrus' father is a good illustration of this doctrine of dissimulation. He posed as a Shiite Muslim in order to do business in the bazaar when he was an agnostic at best. He also covered for his son's acceptance of Christianity. Cyrus was caught up in the Iranian web of manipulation and opportunism. In talking to me about his uncle's theft of his father's inheritance, he castigated Iranians as cheaters and exploiters. Cyrus warded off the manipulative actions of his mother in her attempts to arrange a marriage with his cousin. He bribed his way through the mazeway of military and educational bureaucracies to obtain his visa in order to leave the country. It is interesting to note, however, that Cyrus broke from the behavioral pattern of dissimulation by acknowledging his decision to become a Christian. At least his parents knew of it, and he didn't attempt to conceal it from them. He admitted that his emotional needs were met by Christian missionaries at a crucial time in his life, yet, once in Tehran he became his "own Christian" and established his own life-style.

Perhaps Cyrus' life story may be seen more clearly if one observes the events of change in the world around him. He was born at the conclusion of World War II, after the twenty year reign of Reza Shah Pahlavi who attempted to bring Iran into the modern world, and while allied forces continued to occupy the country. His early childhood occurred during the period of instability under the young king, Mohammed Reza Shah Pahlavi. Cyrus left home to be on his own at about the time of the beginning of the king's "White Revolution." During Cyrus' early years massive Western influences had penetrated Iran in the forms of technicians and technocrats, English language institutes, the American Peace Corps, and the material "goodies" of the West. The influences of the West were evident in school curriculum, Western style of dress, and the mass media filled with Western idioms and images. When Cyrus arrived in the huge city of Tehran, he saw government buildings, embassies, and language and cultural centers of America, England, France, Germany, Italy, and Russia. He rode escalators in department stores and viewed mannequins in British suits and Italian shoes. He walked past cinemas whose marquees displayed bare-breasted women in the arms of a "he-man." Churches, synagogues, universities, colleges, foreign automobiles, and a thousand other novel sights greeted a small-town boy. It was in this environment that Cyrus spent some twelve years of his life separated from his family. Here, in a changing and ambivalent Iran, he turned from adolescence into adulthood.

Often, I have reflected over the life of this young man. And although I have seen the vibrant possibilities for self-development in many Iranian youth, never have I seen the visibility of change enacted with such deliberate speed as in the experiences of Cyrus. For him it appeared that dramatic change was in the atmosphere. I glance at his mother who portrays so perfectly the Islamic pattern of ritual, organization, and fatalism. For her, the one phrase, above all phrases, was "Enshallah," if God wills. For her fate implied uncertainty about future events and the unpredictability of life, so let God do as he willed. It is important to live today for life may be brief and death may be near. So his mother whipped Cyrus into shape, organized his life to schedule as much as she could, and charted his direction, all under "Enshallah." What was impossible for her was change, any change, from the traditional pattern of the past. But she loved Cyrus and often cried over him.

And the father. He espoused no religion, though he used religion for manipulative purposes. He favored change and even encouraged it in the social values of his children. In a real sense he was a man of the present more than he was a man oriented toward the past or the future. He was an enabler. I would guess that he might have been anxious and dissatisfied with the way he lived but was incapable of changing it. Yet he was prepared to make a way for his children to become involved in a future different from what could be his own.

So Cyrus developed a world view, an attitude toward life, and a pattern of behavior that was open to the future and that gave a positive value for coping with the conditions surrounding him. He did not resign himself to life; he was open to all of life's possibilities. He became relatively autonomous with regard to fixed authority, including that of his father, and he developed a considerable capacity for adaptation and innovation to new situations.

And what about Christianity and its influence upon him? Long before Cyrus met Christian missionaries, he had set his face, his tongue, his mind, his heart, and his feet to the tunes of a different drummer. Visions of "sugar plums" had danced in his head. He sensed a change in life opportunities for a small-town boy, in the notions of what he might hope for, work for, reach for. Even if he had to escape to realize those opportunities.

I think the Christian missionaries served as agents of change for him. Cyrus desperately needed love and acceptance at that period of his life, and they showered him with it. The law of Christian love superseded the law of Islamic ritual and fatalism. The missionaries set him on the road to fluency in the English language which, in itself, served as a tremendous medium of change. The fellowship of the church provided him a feeling of warmth where he had experienced much coldness in his family relationships. These Christians had a network of influence which enabled Cyrus to leave his home and enter a new life in Tehran. It is difficult, if not nearly impossible, in a predominantly Muslim setting, for an individual to admit and practice his newly gained faith. Often, if it is done, it is done in dissimulation. Cyrus was sent to a cosmopolitan city to be nurtured in the Christian life where the anonymity of the city provided protection for the deviant person and the minority group.

Cyrus' Christian faith served also as an agent to change. When he became confused in Tehran from the deluge of various Christian groups and their policies, he made certain changes, but he did not change his religion. He did not revert to Islam. He held to his Christian faith in the new commandment of love which was announced by Jesus Christ. Cyrus was always appreciative of the mystery of the faith in his life, and he never bothered to attempt to provide rationalizations for his change of faith, of community, and of life commitment.

One Iranian writer has pointed out three ideals which he asserts underlie the changes occurring in Iran: the dedication to the cult of nationalism begun by Reza Shah and continued by his son; the desire to assert this nationalism by rapid adoption of the material advances of the West; and the breakdown of the traditional power of religion, and the growing tendency toward secularism which came as a result of the first two of these ideals. In this young man Cyrus, we see the influences of all these tendencies. But as Cyrus rides the jet from the country of magic carpets to what he considers his land of promise, he goes as one beating his drum to a tune of mystery.

5 The Stillness of the Wind

It takes a lot of voice for the hawkers of foods and fads to penetrate the walls of the houses along the street. The vegetable or fruit seller pushing his cart has mastered this art, however, for his voice has enough force at 7:00 A.M. to flow over the twelve foot walls, through the yard, under the cracks of doors or through open windows, and sound the alarm of another new day. A hundred and one voices greet the pedestrian on any normal morning's walk. There is no shyness on the street. The blind accordion and tambourine players, in groups of three sticking to one another like glue for fear of being separated, sing their singsong words as they play their aged and dull instruments for hoped-for coins. You can pick up anything in two blocks of some streets, and you may leave the street as you entered it, still colorful and noisy.

The Iranian vocal cord is stretched the greatest, however, in the middle of the street at the time of a car accident. When two cars collide, whether damage is great or small, it is a social occasion, and an instantaneous crowd gathers. And there on the spot, as if by magic, you have a judge, a jury, and a judgment. The two drivers shout, wave arms, gnash teeth, hiss, and often push and shove each other. Absolutely no timidity is observed in the drama. The crowd, somehow nurtured to evenly take sides, edges behind its champion, and a shouting match between the two drivers and their rooters occurs. Finally, a policeman casually strolls up and settles the matter according to the edge of the crowd who shouts the loudest, or takes them off to court. Usually, a bribe takes care of all the injuries. I believe the car accident gives the individual Iranian and also the public at large a chance to vent some of the deepest frustrations of their lives. I would go one step further. I confidently believe that Iranian drivers pull off more revolutions and coups d'etat in their driving habits than the authorities can ever manage or control. They really cannot get at parliament, or the palaces, or the king, or the thousand other persons and places where they would like to vent their hostilities. So the car, the street, other cars, innocent sheep, or poor pedestrians are the targets. Seldom have I seen anyone killed or seriously injured, but there is a battle in the streets night and day.

The Iranian speaks most loudly when the consequences for him are the least threatening. This truth was brought home to me one day while I awaited a flight to Tehran in the Meshed airport. The city of Meshed is the holiest city in Iran. The eighth Imam is buried there in a gold-domed shrine, and hundreds of thousands of pilgrims visit the shrine each year. In fact, many Shiite Muslims make this pilgrimage in lieu of the one to Mecca. Meshed is also the provincial capital for the outlying regions where Omar Khayyam and Ferdowsi lived and wrote.

An Iranian friend, a university student, and I were walking around the balcony of the airport lounge. As I looked down, a pattern of people presented themselves to me. They were stationed in little groups, in circles, chitchatting in low tones. I remarked to my friend how peaceful and placid they looked and sounded. He told me they were talking serious business and desired that no one overhear them. I could not vouch for the content of their conversations, but they spoke in soft voices and they controlled their group from outside interference by the circle. I know for a fact that whenever my friend talked to me of serious matters, whether it was of economics, politics, or social life in general, he lowered his voice, often to a whisper. When I asked him why he did this, he responded that there were listening ears in the walls of the room.

Any voyager in Iran should know one fact of existence within the country. Iranians are socialized through various channels to believe that agents of the secret police are represented among the mullahs, the street sweepers, the newspaper sellers, the taxi drivers, students, teachers, a husband, a wife, a corner grocery operator, the shrine attendant, the shoe-keeper of the mosque, and the maid. In other words, security agents are imagined to sprout from the tree limbs, the blades of grass, the rocks of walls, and the stones of the street. Whether there are few or many agents is unknown. What is known is that people are deeply and daily aware of the possibility of the presence of these persons and their behavior is emphatically controlled by this belief.

I have been engaged in far more whispering conversations than in shouting ones, not that my friends or I were talking subversively but their suspicions of intrusions on all levels of life have caused them to be cautious. Among literate and more educated Iranians, there is the expressed idea that the American CIA years ago trained the domestic spying agency to be one of the most effective outfits in the world. They claim that the Iranian people have been crippled by the fear and suspicion of one another which has been inculcated within them by the security forces. There is no doubt in my mind that I was suspected of being a CIA agent on numerous occasions by various people.

And so there is the anomaly of the highly volatile and expressive Iranian personality caught in the web of suspicion and fear which makes him weak and timid in the crucial areas of his individual and social life where decisions and actions vitally affect him. There is much wind that blows in Iran, but there is an uncanny stillness to its currents.

Mullah Reza's invitation to attend the lecture still stood, so on the appointed evening I was off by taxi to his mosque and the lecture hall which his trustee had so proudly donated to the Muslim community. That day was the birthday of Imam Reza, the eighth Shiite Imam who was buried in Meshed. The taxi driver was surprised to learn of my destination and quizzed me of my reasons for attending the mosque. I explained to him that I was interested in religion in general and more specifically about Islam. I told him that I was a Christian and that I was eager to learn what Muslims thought about the prophet Jesus Christ. He assured me that Muslims honored their prophet Mohammed. However, I raised the question with him why did the prophet speak so highly of Jesus in the Qur'an, more so than he did of himself or the other prophets of the Old Testament. He appeared puzzled at that statement. As we neared the mosque, I asked him of whom did he think more highly, Mohammed, Ali, or Husain. He answered that since he was an uneducated man, he could not read the Qur'an which said great things of Mohammed. He honored Mohammed for his great leadership of Islam. But Ali and Husain were more personal to him, because they helped him in his troubles. Then he said, "My people really pray to Husain when they are in great difficulty."

As the taxi approached the mosque, I could see a birthday atmosphere. People were streaming through the entrance like a stateside crowd going to a football stadium. Strings of lights covered the entrance to the courtyard as well as along the outside walls. The lights provided a carnival effect to it all. There were more lights strung all over the courtyard and on the walls of the mosque and lecture hall. Lights and their symbolic effects were borrowed from the Zoroastrians as the Muslims came into Iran. So on every religious occasion, whether it be Zoroastrian, Muslim, or Christian, lights are utilized in full force. The government has also permanently installed strings of colored light bulbs on most of its buildings so that on national holidays the city is lit up in colorful brilliance. On this night the lights were burning for the birthday of Imam Reza.

I passed through the courtyard where bookstalls were manned by young men selling books, pamphlets, and trinkets, many concerning the life and deeds of Imam Reza. Men were sitting by the pool in meditation. Groups of men were scattered over the courtyard engaged in conversations as they sat in circles on the concrete slabs. I noticed chadored women entering a classroom off to one side of the courtyard. They would hear the lecture over the piped-in intercom system. I was a little early, and seeing no one I knew among the several hundred already gathered, I went to the area between the mosque and the lecture hall, where the shoe-keeper minds the shoes. He was behind his counter and recognizing me from my previous visit he lifted the gate to the shoe-bin and invited me to come sit on an elevated stool beside him. This must have been some sight—an American professor sitting beside the shoe-keeper as people came and went, depositing and receiving their shoes as they prayed in the mosque.

Several young university students approached me across the counter, and speaking in good English, they engaged me in conversation. They desired to tell me of their interest in existentialism and Jean Paul Sartre. I was somewhat surprised for I reckoned that the foremost thought among the worshipers that evening was the birthday of Saint Reza. And it seemed a bit vulgar to discuss this kind of philosophy at a mosque, at a shoestall where shoes were deposited for holy matters. And I was a stranger at that. Quickly I realized that this was only an opening for the students who were eager to inform me of the lecturer's expertise on the subject of Sartre, and how they followed the lecturer from place to place to sit at his feet. By this time the crowds had begun to form at the lecture hall doors, for the evening prayers had concluded, and soon it would be time for the lecture.

Mullah Reza spotted me on my high-stooled seat, and rescued me from my capture and from the stares of hundreds of men who must have wondered, at seeing me behind the counter, if they were at the right place. He had the shoe-keeper unlock the wide doors to the lecture hall and led me into the spacious six hundred seat room, closing the doors behind him.

"We have a special seat reserved for you beside the lecture stand," he said smilingly. "You are our honored guest, and we are glad that you came on this night of the birthday of Imam Reza. This is a good sign for all of us, and the Saint will be happy tonight." He excused himself to attend to last minute details and left me alone in the hall, behind locked doors with muffled sounds outside.

A thousand thoughts rushed through my head as I sat in stillness, alone, on the brink of something happening. The room actually looked like a sanctuary on the style of a Southern Baptist church. Instead of pews there were chairs. The main floor gradually descended to a platform-podium which was elevated by several steps. A balcony, with drapes closed, covered about one-third of the main floor space. A public address system with several microphones was installed on the podium. I wondered what the transition was like for the men to come from the mosque to the hall, from a simple, more Middle Eastern structure where they sat on the floor, to one which seemed too modern with fine chairs, from a mambar to a platform.

Would the occasion be a happy one, celebrating a saint's birthday, or would there be talk of the suffering of the saints? And how would the men view me, sitting in the chair of honor for all to see? The more I sat alone, the more ready I was to blow the candles out and rush home.

Soon, the key turned and a flood of men swept into the room, the first wave taking the front row seats and the others filling the hall progressively to the rear. In no time at all the entire hall was filled, including the balcony whose curtains had been opened. Usually the women sit in the balcony with the curtains drawn in order to segregate them from the men, but not on this occasion. The women were relegated to a classroom to hear the lecture over the public address system. The crowd was representative of a variety of people, from merchants to teachers to students. Many of the young boys sat around the walls and the platform. The room became so crowded that boys were sitting at my feet and the doors were locked to prevent others from entering the hall. I estimated that there were some eight hundred men within the hall, not counting other men in the courtyards and the women in the nearby classroom. Certainly these people were eager to hear something.

I must have given the Persian greeting hundreds of times as I said "Salaam" to those who passed by or who looked or nodded their heads at me from their seats. I knew I was the center of attraction and I played the part to perfection. On these occasions, I had learned one must sit erect, look serious, and without bending the back, nod and bow with head and back in the same plane of movement to those who greet you; at the same time holding your left hand over your chest. I must admit that I enjoyed the moments of Persian hospitality and Braswell ego needs. After all, I had been quite apprehensive moments before. One of the trustees of the mosque who had greeted me earlier announced to the crowd his apologies that there were no more seats and hoped that those in the courtyard and classrooms would be comfortable. He requested that there be no smoking in the hall.

Suddenly, the doors opened and Mullah Reza escorted Dr. Morteza and a young man to the platform. They paused in front of me while the mullah introduced the lecturer to me. He wore no mullah garb, just a plain dark suit with an open white shirt and sandals. He was short of stature with graying hair, and he looked to be about fifty. They took their seats on the platform. One of the trustees sat next to me and informed me that Dr. Morteza had been lecturing in the hall for eight consecutive Friday evenings. When I inquired if the crowds had been similar, he said the hall had been filled to capacity each evening. And then the trustee shocked me with the news that Dr. Morteza had been imprisoned several times for anti-government statements, especially as he preached against the neglect of the government in attending to the social and physical needs of the people. In fact he said that Dr. Morteza had just been released from prison several months ago. I thought to myself, "What a birthday party this will be if this place is raided." In Iran you are guilty until proven innocent.

After the mullah made the introductions, the young man came to the podium and chanted a portion of the Qur'an in Arabic with rhythmic and clear enunciation as only one trained can do. Then, the trustee who was the donor of the hall recited in Persian a poem which he had composed especially for the birthday of the saint. Now it was time for the lecturer. Dr. Morteza spoke for an hour and a half on the history and personality of Imam Reza. His oratory was spellbinding on the crowd as he narrated with rhythmic soft and loud tones, gesticulating with fingers, head, and arms. He certainly lit the candles in praise of the saint. But there was more, and the more was hot.

Dr. Morteza spoke of the teachings of all the Imams upon the importance of both matter and spirit in Islam. "What advantage is it to a man to pray if he doesn't have bread?" he asked his audience who by this time were on the edge of their seats. "It is foolish to expect a man to pray who hasn't eaten the food necessary to give him the energy to live and pray. If a person hurts because he has an empty stomach, or has been mistreated, it is natural to express his pain by uttering a cry. When one cries, it is quite obvious that one is suffering. When one suffers, he is compelled to find a remedy for it." Dr. Morteza admonished the younger generation to find ways to alleviate sufferings and bring hope to Iranian people.

There it was—Persian dissimulation at its best. Dr. Morteza had spoken on themes of deprivation, oppression, and hostility, and had found a format to express them on the occasion of Imam Reza's birthday. These were indeed anti-political establishment ideas which were veiled in the festivities of a birthday party. Surely, there were eyes and ears in the audience if not in the very walls. I expected a raid as if I were in some illegal X rated movie house. But it didn't come and I was glad. I could envision in the headlines, "American Missionary-Professor Apprehended At Lecture."

As Dr. Morteza concluded his lecture he led the men in prayers, especially praying that all Muslims would be victorious over the Jews in Israel. He also prayed that the prisoners in jails would be liberated; I suppose he meant Iranian jails. Then, he came to my seat and sat down beside me as attendants served us hot chocolate and cookies. It was the first time I had been served anything except tea. There was food for all in the courtyard, and the crowd began making their way outside. Dr. Morteza and I had little time for conversation because young people milled around us, asking questions, staring, and listening. He invited me to come visit him in his office and I gladly accepted.

As I departed the hall Mullah Reza placed six bags of candy in my hands to share with my family in commemoration of the saint's birthday. As he escorted me through the courtyard we passed groups of men eating and drinking and browsing around the bookstalls amid a thousand colored lights canopying the courtyard. Women, too, in their tightly drawn chadors, stood with their husbands. It was evident that these people had really enjoyed themselves on this Friday evening. I had too, but I wondered about it all. I wanted to hear more from Dr. Morteza.

His office was as busy as a beehive with young men boxing books as I entered it the next day. We had to talk in whispers as the students and office workers obviously stood close by to overhear our conversations. He told me that his father was a mullah, and that he had studied under his father and had taught Islamic subjects in various schools in Iran, including several colleges. Now he was a publisher, teacher, editor, and lecturer who went to cities and villages over the country, lecturing on Islam in universities, mosques, bazaars, schools, homes, and lecture halls. With a university group he might discuss some of the relationships of the philosophies and psychologies of Freud, Camus, Jung, or Sartre to Islam, analyzing their contributions to understanding man, and criticizing their misunderstanding of man in the light of Islamic teaching. He said he liked to speak to the illiterate and uneducated on the lives and personalities of the great Shiite Imams who were martyrs to the cause of truth.

During our conversation he continued to talk in whispers. When I asked him about Islamic reform movements in Iran, he said there were none and changed the subject. It appeared to me that he was over guarded in his words with me. During our conversation a mullah entered the office who had an appointment with him. As I was introduced to him, I recalled hearing him over the radio during a holy season observance in which he offered prayers in behalf of the king's health and safety. I thought it rather strange that here were two men who seemingly participated in two different "Islamic loyalties," one who had served prison terms for his criticism of high persons in high places, and one who had uttered prayers on a government sponsored radio station in behalf of the king and the powers that be. I would like to have overheard their conversation.

I returned home that day, as I had returned the night before after listening to Dr. Morteza; I reflected on the puzzles before me. Although he had not named a single individual or any single agency, he had been quite critical of the leadership of Iran. Whereas Mullah Kareem much earlier at his home had indicated his loss of pulpit because of his words of criticism, Dr. Morteza was able to cover the territory with his "veiled" preachments. And yet, no mob scene developed at the mosque to march in protest and demand change. No heckler stood up to defend or to deny his statements. And why would such a safe and nice mosque like that of Mullah Reza invite a speaker with a prison record like Dr. Morteza? It just all seemed so enigmatic to me. I had often heard the adage, "Sticks and stones may bruise my bones, but words will never harm me." But words are forces for change, I thought. In Christian terms, the Word became flesh, took force, lived, enacted a drama for change, and effected that change in the lives of millions. And yet, in circle after circle of mullahs and teachers and students and people in general, words are rushed into dead-ends. Words are spoken and fall into cups of tea. The wind blows, and there is an uncanny silence to it all. Surely, this is my problem being a foreigner in a strange land. But I will still pursue the wind and its stillness.

I was really involved in the wind currents of a theological debate one evening in the south of the city. A student friend's uncle was a mullah of a mosque, and his uncle invited us to a Qur'anic study meeting in the home of one of his members. The host, a bazaar merchant, met us at the door and led us into the living room filled with thirty-five men seated on the floor and leaning their backs against the walls of the room. An elderly man, from pure and unflawed memory, beautifully chanted verses from the Qur'an while the others responded in praise to Allah. I was seated on a large cushion next to what appeared to me to be a throne chair with its legs cut off. I surmised that the chair was for the mullah. The host introduced me and then counseled the group to repeat their sayings slowly so that I might follow them. He didn't know that I had no knowledge of the Arabic language, but I could understand their translations into Persian.

After thirty minutes of chanting and recitations, Mullah Abdol appeared with his son-in-law and nephew. He was a jolly round man with a snow-white beard, a white turban, and a deep black robe. He left his sandals at the door and walked directly to his throne chair, greeting me with the head nod and arms crossed against his chest. Every man had arisen to bow before him as he took his seat. Surprisingly to me, he immediately asked his son-in-law, Mahmud, to speak. Mahmud was a graduate in social sciences from the University of Tehran and fluent in English. Mahmud quickly asserted to the men that Islam was concerned with three things—faith, reason, and knowledge. He went on to say that the result of Imam Husain's revolution was not simply beating chests and crying, but it was to put into practice all the truths of the Qur'an.

An older man, wearing a green headdress signifying that he was a Hajji (a pilgrim of Mecca), interrupted Mahmud and in an angry voice accused him of attacking the cherished beliefs and practices of his fathers. Mahmud remained very calm while the older man became more vocal and heated in his remarks. It was an amazing encounter for me. In the first place I was surprised that the mullah called upon his son-in-law who was so youthful to address such an older group who were obviously from the bazaar district which is the most conservative domain of Islamic practice. I also was taken aback that Mahmud would address himself to such a negative appraisal of a cherished form of Shiite obedience. Many of my university students had discussed the old-fashioned ways of chest beating and crying and wished for their demise. But that was in private conversation. I could not imagine a young man saying such things to his elders, especially in the presence of a mullah, and his father-in-law at that Shortly, there was a buzzing of voices all around the room to disrupt the exchange between the two. This continued for a few minutes until Mullah Abdol said in a firm and loud voice, "It is enough!" And turning to the host, he said, "Please serve the tea." Once again tea had rescued the situation. But more than tea was the respect that the men had toward their mullah in simmering down their feelings.

While we all drank tea, the mullah read passages from the Qur'an, first in Arabic, then in Persian in order for me to understand. The gist of his interpretations of the scriptures was to have a good knowledge of Allah, to live a good moral life with no lying and stealing, and to treat a man like you would treat Allah. It was obvious that Mullah Abdol was not an orator. He was a teacher and seemed to have the heart of a pastor. As he spoke the only sound beside his own was the occasional sip of tea through the sugar cube held between the teeth of each one of us.

In my unpreparedness my time of fire had come, and I wanted to hide. The mullah looked at me as I sat beside him, mentioned to the men that I was a learned professor, and asked me to speak. The debate had hardly simmered down when I was called on to say something to this group of pious and faithful Muslims. My halting words stumbled out something like this. "Mr. Abdol and my good friends, I thank you for your kindness in inviting me to your Qur'anic meeting tonight. In my church we have similar meetings to study the Bible. Your distinguished mullah is a man of great wisdom and learning, and he has mentioned the light of the prophet and the Imams which is passed down through the ages to give each of you knowledge and wisdom. In my religion we believe that Jesus Christ, a prophet whom you honor very highly, is the light of God to the world. I am glad that we can both talk about the gift of light, because there is much darkness all around us."

I wanted to say something that would be appropriate for the occasion, that would demonstrate my own religious background, and would stimulate them to discussion. I certainly did not want to be offensive and initiate another heated argument. Looking at Mullah Abdol, I asked, "What is the light like that comes from your prophet and the Imams." I knew that Iranian Shiites believed that their twelfth Imam would return someday to overcome evil and restore the right and the good. The mullah reflected for a moment and answered, "It is a light of wisdom and courage that few are willing to follow. The light has led our Imams to martyrdom, but it has never been extinguished. Jesus brought the light also but people were not receptive, and that is why we have our prophet and the Imams."

The host had come to whisper something in the mullah's ear and closing the Qur'an in his lap he led the men in the familiar prayers for the sick and the imprisoned. The prayers served as a signal for the men's departure, and they said farewell to me and the mullah as they filed past our seats. The old gentleman who had argued so violently earlier smiled at me as he passed and paused and said, "Will you become a Muslim?" I returned the smile and answered,

"If you will not make me beat my chest." He seemed to get the point as he moved out the door. I nudged my friend that we should go for it was 10 P.M., and I looked around for Mullah Abdol. But we were not to leave for another hour, for the host had invited us to stay for a full meal with the mullah and his kin.

The host spread a tablecloth in the middle of the room, covering the finely woven silk carpet. Mullah Abdol had gone to the bathroom to wash, and on returning to the room it was obvious that he had removed his turban for it was tilted to one side. Mahmud quickly jumped up from the floor and corrected it. The host served us plates heaped with Iranian rice, fish, various meat-sauce toppings for the rice, and bowls of fruit. There was to be no talking during the meal, for it was evident that they were famished, and food was more appropriate for the mouth than words. I used a fork, but not the mullah. He used his fingers just as skillfully as I used my fork, and more so, to funnel the food into his mouth. Not a woman of the house appeared during the entire meal, nor did the host sit to eat with us. He busied himself scurrying back and forth from the kitchen with the hot food.

I felt free enough after the meal to ask Mullah Abdol if the argument during the study meeting was abnormal. He told me that Iranian men were seldom bashful, and that since all the men present considered themselves expert in the teachings of the Qur'an, they each wanted to tell their opinions about all matters. Mahmud spoke up, "We must be honest to tell you that in Iran men are not bashful but they have become more silent. There is not in all of Iran today a famous mullah who is free to speak to the people. All of these men have been prohibited from speaking from the mambar. I could tell you name after name of scholars and religious leaders who have spoken out and have been silenced. Mosques and lecture halls have been closed."

"But what about your challenge to the elder man in the meeting?" I asked. Mahmud glanced at his father-in-law as if to get permission to continue speaking and said, "For a long time our people have cried to the Imams and have beat their chests in desperation out of the sadness of their life and their hope for a good life in the future. We must express our feelings or we will die, but we must think of a better way to bring change to our lives. Imam Husain's revolution was a positive one based on the teachings of the Qur'an, and our prophet Mohammed, and Imam Ali. It is true that Imam Husain was killed in the process of establishing the principles of Islam, but we must not cry over him the rest of our lives. We must honor him with positive programs for the welfare of our people."

Mullah Abdul had remained strangely silent. It was getting late and he had grown tired from a full day. I myself felt sleepy after such a large meal at such a late hour. Mahmud offered to give us a ride home which we gladly accepted, for taxis in that part of the city were difficult to find at late hours. The host graciously received our thanks as we departed, and I imagine the women of the household rushed in to clean up the disarray which had resulted from some three hours of tea drinking, cigarette smoking, and food eating. Enough had been said to again remind me of the difficulty of speech both among the men of the cloth as well as among Muslims in general. It appeared to me that it was easier for the men to speak about the ultimate than it was for them to talk about the mundane. Again, I observed the stillness of the wind.

Mullahs and mosques and Muslims like Mahmud might be expected to demonstrate a certain quietude because of the tensions between their religious expectations and the political realities of the day. But the spirit of careful conservatism was evident among all groups of Iranians, including the various sectarian expressions of the Christian church. Long ago in the Middle East when Islamic leaders overran Christian controlled territories, they allowed Christians, as well as other religious groups, to live and rule over their own affairs within certain geographic boundaries, called mellats. Christians learned to survive as minorities quite well by paying particular respect to the sultan or the king. They learned to trade off taxes and obedience for peace and life in their own sections of the village or city. Iran was no different. In the sixteenth century, for example, King Shah Abbas, whose capital city Isfahan rivaled London and Paris as cultural centers of the day, delivered thousands of Armenian Christians from the oppression of the Turks and gave them a quarter of the city to live in and become his artisans. Christians have fared admirably well under Muslim rulership in Iran, for they have learned, I believe, to pay unto Caesar and to God what are their dues. After all, this is the politics of life between the plurality and the wee minority. It was not so with the Baha'is in the nineteenth century. They threatened the Iranian rulership with menacing theological and political ideas and behavior, and were consequently persecuted and denied a legitimate expression in the country.

Iranian Christians, then, know their place and the peripheries of it, just as do their Jewish and Zoroastrian neighbors. There is something peculiar about the Christian communities in Iran, particularly the Protestant ones. They are something of pariah groups, especially those who have had American missionary activities in the country. This is not to say that all Iranian Christian groups have become somewhat subservient upon more economically affluent and personnel trained foreign church agencies. In particular the Assyrian Church of the East and the Armenian Orthodox Church have been indigenous expressions of Christianity in Iran for centuries. But the more recent Protestant Iranian churches founded by American and European missionaries have depended to a great extent upon their founders for leadership and monies. These Western-influenced Protestant Christians have had to consider two dilemmas in their Christian stance in the country. They could not offend their donors who were their lifeline for men and material to build their church, and they had to tread softly in overwhelmingly Muslim soil where the Christian gospel was an affront. So there are ample historical and sociological reasons for the quietude of the

Iranian Christian Church.

The stillness of the wind continues to be a most interesting experience to observe in the breezes that blow and die in Iran. One of the most disturbing and pathetic experiences I had while in the country was to witness the continual dying out of the Zoroastrian community. King Cyrus was said to know the Zoroastrian god, Ahura Mazda, even some two thousand and five hundred years ago. Zoroastrians with their fire altars and high monotheism reigned in Iran until the Islamic invasions in the seventh century A.D. It is now said that they number less than fifty thousand in their native soil. Through persecution, retrenchment, and migration these noble people of good thought, good word, and good deed have also entered their extreme stillness.

If there is stillness in an uncanny abundance of activity among mullahs and mosques, and if the wind currents have yet to truly spawn a whirlwind among the more ancient, and more recent Christians, and if the winds have nigh ceased to blow for the Zoroastrians, there is yet plenty of wind blowing in Iran which strangely still is an amalgam of both old and modern Persia.

6 A Season of Obedience

In the cold winter months in Tehran snow covers the visible peak of Mount Damavand, some seventy-five miles to the north, as it rises nineteen thousand feet above sea level. Snow also comes to this sprawling city of four million inhabitants, and its one snow plow is just not enough to cope with the wide boulevards and narrow alleyways. Once, I parked my four cylinder car for two weeks because snow chains were selling for one hundred dollars a pair. Besides, it is warmer to ride the two-decker buses imported from England in cold weather when body to body heat in the sardine packed interior provides a counterattack against the cold air currents that sweep down from Russia and the Caspian Sea area. It is in the buses that the chadored women draw tighter their coverings from the stares of the men and where three cents can take you within the Iranian world.

But ice, snow, and cold breezes do not keep Muslims from their obedience season. And these hazardous conditions certainly do not keep the blind beggars away from their favorite street corners. "Allah bless you," they respond at your passing, in anticipation of your obedience in jingling some coins in their outstretched, cold hands. "May your hand never hurt you," they sing, when you place a coin in those numb hands.

But what about these blind men? I never pass them without

thinking of the blind men in St. Luke's gospel. Jesus passed a blind man in the street who reached out begging for sight, as Jesus set his face toward Jerusalem, the city of hope and death. The disciples, who couldn't or didn't understand this necessary pilgrimage to Golgotha by Jesus, reprimanded the blind man by telling him to shut up or get back on his street corner. The blind man had been begging for years waiting to receive a little change. But Jesus came to his home territory, his street corner, and he shouted the words that pricked the ears of Jesus, "Son of David," and Jesus gave him sight right there, and the beggar became light and life.

And Jesus moved on to that city, Jerusalem, the city whose obedience is so carefully measured today, where the Jew wails at the wailing wall which represents the restoration of the kingdom; where the Muslim yearns to worship at the Dome of the Rock where his prophet Muhammed's flight to heaven occurred and is hallowed ground; where the Christian knows so much of the ministry of Jesus, Golgotha, the empty tomb, and Pentecost.

These blind beggars have staked out their territory in these wintry months in the streets among the pedestrians, bicycles, four-wheelers, veiled women, and fruit hawkers. And the coins jingle in their hands, for it is a time of obedience, for almsgivers gain special merit as they warm the cold palms with money. I would give them money too, not for merit, though I guess I needed that too if I believed their system, but it hurt me to see them, still, alone, and facing darkness.

I came to know one blind man in this land of King Cyrus and the Magi, of Persian carpets and black gold, of the symbols of light and darkness which the Zoroastrians so shared with their Jewish and Christian neighbors. The winter months are the obedience season for Muslims. Though the months of special Islamic observances may vary according to the Islamic lunar calendar, this particular month of December is the season of Ramazan, the fasting month. During this season every good Muslim must fast from sunup to sundown. The obedient Muslim takes neither food nor water in these daylight hours, and one does not participate in other bodily pleasures. It is a time when some become extremely agitated over minor matters, for their stomachs growl and their patience threshold is low. January is the month when faithful Muslims make the sacred pilgrimage (hajj) to Mecca in Saudi Arabia which is the ultimate sign of obedience in their religion. In February in the mosques and homes they have worship and prayer meetings in which they cry for the tragedy of their Imam Husain, and cry for the return of their twelfth Imam.

But for December, obedience is demonstrated in fasting. Late in the afternoon of a December day, the snow was lightly falling. I was lecturing to a class of Muslim seminarians with their white turbans twirled high on their heads and their long, flowing, black robes draped over their erect bodies. It was somewhat miraculous that I was a visiting professor in this all-Muslim seminary. The dean of the faculty had invited me to teach world religions if I would agree not to proselytize his preacher boys. As the sun began to set, the seminarians became restless, not from their lectures of course, but from the hunger pains and growls of their empty stomachs. We could hear the call from the minaret, the prayer tower of the nearby mosque, summoning the millions of Muslims to prayer and the breaking of the fast for the day. "Professor, it is time to break the fast with prayer and food," interrupted a young Muslim preacher. "We have had no food or water for fifteen hours." I had been lecturing on the prophet Jesus' teachings on grace. And even though we had covered only one hour of a two-hour class on world religions, I was not about to have another crusade on my hands. As surely as I would cause a riot if their wishes were not granted, as well as being discourteous to them, I nodded in agreement and dismissed class.

The more zealous prayers and eaters broke from the room in their flowing robes; the more zealous missionary students remained behind, two in number, and gently closed the classroom door. One of them looked me in the eye and said, "You are aware that you are a polytheist when you worship the three gods of your religion. We worship Allah, the one God of the Old Testament, and the New Testament, and of the Qur'an, and of the whole world."

I thought to myself, "This is not fair; they are attempting to proselytize me on their home territory." And besides, my hands had been tied by the dean not to attempt to personally persuade any of the students toward my religious faith. Well, they had opened up a complicated topic in the concept of the Trinity. But they had really remained behind for another purpose. The other seminarian spoke. He was blind from birth. I knew his life history, for over cups of Iranian tea he had told me of his pilgrimage through life. Mr. Mohammadi was the preacher of a mosque in faraway Abadan, the city of the largest oil refinery in the world, located on the Persian Gulf. He had made a special arrangement with me for class attendance, one week in Abadan with his family and work, and one week in Tehran in the seminary. He was the train commuter par excellence. He had made the pilgrimage to Mecca several times in hopeful obedience that Allah would restore his sight. But to no avail. "It must be Allah's fate," he had often told me.

Now he spoke. "There is no value for me to rush with the others to break the fast with gulps of food. It would be like the blind leading the blind. We blind have a special compensation. We can persevere. Have you ever heard a blind beggar on the streets complain that his hands were cold?" He had a point as far as I was concerned, for I couldn't recall that I had.

Then he placed his hand near the warmth of mine, as if the heat were a sensor, and said, "We sense that you are agitated by the early dismissal of the class. But this is our obedience season. Some of us are under a mandate of obedience to do without food all these days in order to share the excess food which we accumulate with those who beg for food on our streets, and in Africa, and around the world. What kind of obedience do you Christians offer?"

The blind preacher's question was a disturbing one. Was it a test of comparison, or maybe a competitive invitation, or possibly a movement of inquisitiveness toward the Christian's prerogatives? The hour was running late for prayers, and Mr. Mohammadi and his friend excused themselves and hastened off, as best a blind man can hasten. For how fast could he go through the snow, much less the traffic congestion? And I just knew what would happen outside the seminary gate, for I had seen the little drama before. Mr. Mohammadi, in no real hurry to break his fast, would reach out for the hand of the perennial blind man who always begged outside our gate and fasten in his hand enough money to buy chelo-kabab for him and his family. The blind giving light and life to the blind on this cold and snowy day. Could this be a little piece of Jerusalem? Very possibly, Jesus was passing by in this season of obedience.

The blind man's gesture as an act of obedience must have been multiplied throughout the city many times, but my cynicism about some of the practices of the Ramazan season still gripped me. I recalled Mullah Abbas' son's visit to my home in which he told me that many Muslims really fake piety during Ramazan. On one occasion he said, "Some of my friends stay up all night eating and then sleep most of the day so they won't be hungry." When I inquired about going to school and work during the season of Ramazan, he responded, "It is really a big holiday for many. School attendance is not carefully measured. Shop keepers understand why their workers come in late. Ramazan is a lazy season in our country."

I, too, had noticed how shops opened quite late during the fasting season and how they closed at dusk for several hours to break the fast. I learned never to go into a corner grocery at fast-breaking time, for there was a stampede to get bread, meat, and drink. And every Ramazan season the streets seemed to be barer of cars and people. So the rhythm of life did change for the month, whether Muslims were serious or not in their observances.

"What about your family schedule?" I asked the mullah's son. "We are not the lazy kind," he smiled. "We awake faithfully when the call to prayer comes from the mosque about 5 A.M. My father really awakens us and we say our individual prayers and think about Allah. About 5:30 A.M. my father goes to the mosque to lead the people in prayers. Sometimes I go with him. Sometimes I go back to sleep, and he awakens me about 8 A.M. to go to work in the bazaar. At noon we all go to the mosque for prayers and a talk by my father on the good habits of the fast. By 6 P.M. when the fast ends for the day, we are all hungry and eat bread and cheese and drink yogurt. Usually, from 7 to 9 P.M. my father leads prayers and discussions in the mosque, and after that time we eat a big meal of rice, meat, and vegetables which my mother has prepared. We usually eat fruit and drink tea into late in the night and just before going to bed we eat the leftovers of the warmed rice and meat. Sometimes we go to sleep and wake up about 4 A.M. to eat the leftovers to carry us through the day. But we absolutely eat nothing in the daylight hours."

"How do you help the needy by doing this?" I teasingly asked. "My father is always giving money and food to the poor," he responded. Well, some obey and some play I had readily learned from the mullah's son. But the blind mullah's act of obedience still passed before my mind and heart.

No sooner does the Ramazan season end than the pilgrimage month begins. The Qur'an commands every believer to make the pilgrimage to Mecca, the holy city of Islam, once in a lifetime if one has the wealth and the health. The prophet Mohammed was born there, and the holy shrine, the Ka'ba, is dedicated to the worship of Allah, and to that shrine every Muslim must come and pray. The journey and completion of the pilgrimage usually takes some thirty days, but the preparation for it may take a lifetime. The pilgrimage, too, is a season of obedience.

In early January, my friend Kasem invited me to his home village to spend the night and to talk with his elderly father who was soon to go on the pilgrimage to Mecca. From my fantasy dreams of Iran in earlier years, I had imagined it to be a hot and dry country. The winters in Tehran, which is in the north, are icy and snowy. But on this night to the south some several hundred miles, I believed myself to be in the arctic zone. The little village was in stark contrast to the big city. The little shops along the dirt streets were one-story affairs, many with earthen floors and doors that pulled down from overhead. One or two old modeled Volkswagens traveled the narrow alleyways, for they were mostly traffiked by sheep and goats.

Kasem's house was a simple one, one large room with carpets on the floor and pillows placed for leaning against the wall, and one small adjoining room for pots, pans, and bedrolls. All over Iran Persian carpets are like bank rolls, and often several carpets may be superimposed on one another, like the floor of Kasem's house. That evening we sat on the floor with cushions to our backs and with blankets drawn tightly around our legs and waists to conserve the heat from the charcoal iron grill beneath the blankets.

His sixty-seven-year-old father, with wrinkled, worn, and prideful face, sat across from me beside his wife in her chador. Several of Kasem's uncles had been invited over to observe this stranger in their village and brother's house. One of the uncles told me that he had never been twenty kilometers outside the village. In fact, that twenty kilometers measured the distance to a "far away" shrine where he visited with his family on several occasions to picnic and offer prayers. Another uncle wanted to fit me with a hat the next day in his hat shop to which I readily agreed. But the occasion that evening was the father's soon-to-be pilgrimage.

He related to me the preparations for the anticipated greatest moment of his life. He told me that he had spent years weaving Persian carpets in order to sell them and save money for such a pilgrimage as this. "My religion requires me to pay all my religious taxes and to save enough money to provide for my family for one year before I go. It takes very much money for the taxes and air ticket and the twenty-five days in Mecca and the gifts which I want to bring my family and friends." I had often heard that at this time of year friends of prospective pilgrims visit them more frequently to insure that their friendship is warm. I asked him about his health. He replied that he was an old man and often experienced fainting spells, but in order to obey his prophet, he must go. "It will be a month of difficult travel, of eating that Arab food, of walking the footsteps of the prophet, of praying, of offering lambs in sacrifice. When I am in Mecca, I will walk side by side with a million pilgrims from all over the world, all in white robes which signify their equality with each other and their unity in brotherhood. Even my Shah shall not be above me in the holy city."

The old man talked eagerly and excitedly about his pilgrimage in obedience, and incessantly expressed his desire to fulfill the will of Allah. With tears in his eyes, he said, "My wife has sewn for me this white robe," as he held it before my view. "It shall be my only garment while I visit the holy city, and it shall be my burial garment if Allah wills that I make the pilgrimage. My wife has promised to bury me in it when I die."

Upon returning from the pilgrimage, he assured me that he would be given the title, hajji, meaning one who had made the hajj, a title of reverence and authority. People of the village would place complete confidence and trust in him as a man of Allah and would seek his counsel on all matters. They would say of him, "He has walked in the house of Allah and has seen his salvation." As he talked I could detect the envy of his brothers as they listened. In Tehran I had met many men called hajji. The title did carry with it a certain religious connotation which people respected. I could just envision his return laden with transitor radios, tape recorders, perfumes, and clothes. I could see his tiny home decorated with flowers which his friends would send him in congratulations, and I could see the lines of people as they filed by to speak a word with him about his pilgrimage. And I could imagine the winter nights right in the room where we were sitting when select men of the village would come and sit under the blankets to hear the tales of the old man's trip of a lifetime.

The evening was late and the brothers left. Kasem's father and mother excused themselves to retire to the smaller room to sleep, leaving the larger room and the charcoal fire for us. But before he left, he paused and said something which I had intuited he would. A lifetime of planning for human destiny was pitted against the answer which he hoped to elicit from me, "Does Christianity have a greater obedience than this?" And in that instance I was reminded of the student preacher's question to me of obedience. Indeed it was obedience time. Again, I thought of the city of Jerusalem and remembered that the old man's prophet Mohammed had early in his life looked in the direction of Jerusalem to offer his prayers. But he had become disenchanted with the Jews of his day, and changed the direction of facing a city to Mecca. And I reflected over Jesus' saying, "Jerusalem, Jerusalem, how often would I have gathered you as a hen gathers her chicks and you would not." It would take another evening to share with the old man the city of Jerusalem, the Mount of Zion, the footstool of God; perhaps when he finished his pilgrimage I might make another journey to the village, maybe at Easter.

No matter which way one looks at it, the pilgrimage is big business. In this particular pilgrimage year, some fifty-eight thousand Iranians were to go to Mecca and spend in excess of ten billion rials (one hundred and forty-five million dollars). Besides Kasem's father I talked with an Iranian schoolteacher who made the journey. Mrs. Amin had lived in Tehran all her life but had made several tours to Europe and America. She classified the hajj as the most meaningful journey of her life. "I was a candidate automatically when my father died and left me an inheritance. In our religion anyone who owns property or investments which exceed the expenses of a hajj must go on it as a religious obligation. It is quite expensive you know. I know a poor woman who has been a servant most of her life. She saved every rial (penny) she could and finally made her pilgrimage."

"What is it like to go to Mecca?" I quizzed her. She was a beautiful woman in her early fifties and quite stately in her mannerisms. "Before I went on the pilgrimage I could have excuses for my sins, but after the journey I could have no excuses. I used to dance, drink, and smoke. Now I am free from those things. Before I went on the pilgrimage I had caused many of my friends much harm through gossip. I went to each one before leaving and asked their forgiveness. While I was in Saudi Arabia, I threw stones at the devil as a part of my pilgrimage and this ensured that I would not commit those same sins against my friends upon my return. One of the most meaningful moments of the entire pilgrimage was as thousands of us stood around the Ka'ba to pray. There we were, rich and poor, the mighty and the weak, from all parts of the world praying together in our white robes. We women were to let our faces show as we marched around the Ka'ba, and I know that for some of the women it was a new experience to show their face in public and especially before men. This is one reason I don't go to mosques, because the men force us women to wear the chador and I will not do it. I can pray just as well at home."

"How did your friends react to you when you returned?" I asked, wondering if women were treated any differently than men. "They respected me more," she replied. "They knew the journey was difficult. It is not a vacation. I forgot the poor facilities and the roughness of the travel. I did not talk about this when I returned as many do, bragging of their hardships. I brought back with me an inner peace, really an inner light, which my students and their parents, and other teachers and friends noticed. Of course they joked and called me Hajjieh Amin, just as they call a man, hajji. But I am a changed person, and they know it."

This lady spoke confidently of her pilgrimage to the holy city, and this impressed me, for I heard that she was one of the best teachers in the city. Her life-style was modern in so many ways, yet in the traditional pilgrimage she was found faithful and obedient. Obedience really was a theme of these winter months.

Both December and January are intense, devotional months for the serious-minded Muslim. I often became exhausted just thinking about the efforts and discipline involved in fasting for a solid month and going on the pilgrimage. But they were doing it, not I. And yet, over and over again, in their friendly ways they were testing their obedience against my own. In a world of hunger the blind preacher was giving another day of light and hope to countless others. And Kasem's elderly father! Even in his old age he was first obedient in caring for his family's needs before going on the greatest obedient trip of his life. And Mrs. Amin in her sophistication and modernity was nevertheless bound to a faithful commitment.

But I must admit that I was never so emotionally drained in my life as the month of February passed. It was Muharram season when Muslims grieved over the death of their spiritual leader. During the first ten days of the month, series of meetings are held in mosques and homes to commemorate the tragedy at Kerbala, Iraq, in the seventh century A.D., when Imam Husain and his family members were slain by dissident Muslims. Husain was the son of Ali and Fatemah and the grandson of the prophet. He became Allah's great martyr, and Iranian Shiite Muslims vicariously identify with him and his family in their deaths at the hands of the "unjust and corrupt" Arab Sunni Muslims.

The city prepares well for these mourning days. Newspapers are filled with announcements of all the special meetings. Radio and television run hours of programs on the Imam. The police caution the storekeepers to refrain from selling alcoholic beverages, which Muslims are not to do in the first place. It is usually those "Armenian Christian shopkeepers" who sell those beverages. The police also ask the cinemas to close. Black flags, symbolizing the mourning period, flutter from every shop in the bazaar, from every mosque in the city, and from the doorways of those houses whose occupants are having prayer meetings in behalf of Imam Husain. And they number into the tens of thousands. Twenty-five gallon water drums line the bazaar streets and main thoroughfares where pedestrians pause to drink a fresh cup of water and offer a prayer to Imam Husain who was denied water by his foes in the battle. The bazaar merchants realize merits from Allah as they hand out cups of water to the people. The solemn and foreboding atmosphere of the city is a turnabout to the festival sights of lights and lightness on occasions of birthday celebrations for the Imams and the king.

On the eighth night of Muharram (the tenth day is Ashura, the day on which Imam Husain was killed along with his family members), Mr. Kashani, a university student friend, took me to a large mosque in the northern section of the city. We passed through the courtyard and arrived at the entrance of the mosque. The shoekeeper had no more space in his shoe racks to place our shoes, so he gave us a cellophane bag in which to place them. We carried them in hand as we sought a place to sit on the floor. I felt like Moses who took off his shoes at the burning bush. Mr. Kashani whispered, "You are on holy ground." With some eight hundred men seated around us shoeless, I wished for a fan in the dead of the winter cold. But it didn't bother them in the least. They were not observing like I was; they had come to worship.

A beautiful bright red Turkoman carpet covered the massive floor. Mosques usually have no pews, or chairs for that matter, and it is the custom of Muslims to sit in a cross-legged position in neat and straight rows. An enormous crystal chandelier hung from the central ceiling, no doubt donated by a pious and wealthy Muslim. Several balconies were evident from my vantage point, one of which was covered by green-colored curtains to segregate the women who were attending. Women may be "kingpins" in the home, but the mosque is the man's world. Toward the central wall a mambar (pulpit) stood, like a scaffold. There were twelve steps which ascended to a green-cushioned seat. Microphones were fastened to the pulpit to carry the words of the preacher to the far corners of the room and to the courtyard outside.

We had arrived late, and the preacher was concluding his sermon. He was perched high on the pulpit, and in a rhythmic tone and movement he was narrating the drama of the Husain story. He described the death of Imam Husain's son in graphic detail and with a breaking voice, choked with emotion. Men began to weep. They brought out handkerchiefs to wipe away the streaming tears from their cheeks and to cover their eyes. The moans of the women from the balcony often drowned out the men's cries. It seemed to me, the only foreigner in the mosque, that they all knew the narrative by heart and cried in harmony as the preacher elicited grief from them. Mr. Kashani whispered to me that we must return the next night to really experience the drama of Husain.

After some fifteen minutes of this narrative and crying, the preacher blessed the crowd with prayer and the meeting concluded. As we left the mosque, Mr. Kashani introduced me to the pastor (Pishnamaz) and the visiting evangelist (Va'ez) who warmly greeted me and invited me to return the following evening. In the courtyard four young men stopped me and asked me if I desired to become a Muslim. I guess that was a natural question since I was the only pale face in a sea of tan Iranians. Why would a stranger come to a place like that unless he were really interested in becoming a Muslim? I remembered how Jesus wept over the death of Lazarus and again over the city of Jerusalem. And cold chills ran down my spine as I freshly recalled the haunting cries and mourns of these Muslims over the death of their saint.

Before I could speak, one of the young men asked me if I had read a certain book by a famous Muslim professor and preacher who, he indicated, was in political prison in Tehran for his preaching. By this time a large crowd had gathered around us, and before I could speak, Mr. Kashani had shoved me through the crowd and into the street to catch a waiting taxi. As we sped wildly downtown, all the time being assured by the driver of our utter safety in his care, I asked Mr. Kashani, "Why did you interrupt our conversation with the young men in the courtyard?" He apologized and said, "We must be careful not to deliver you into the hands of the revolutionaries. These are jittery times in our country. The youth are unsettled. The intellectuals are teaching ideas contrary to the establishment. And the people are crying with more intensity in the mosques. We must be careful."

The next evening, the night before Ashura, Mr. Kashani and I returned to the mosque in northern Tehran early in order to obtain a good seat near the pulpit. In fact, the pastor had invited me to be his guest at a special place near the first step of the pulpit. It was to no avail. I thought something was peculiar because the courtyard was filled. By force we squeezed through the tightly woven crowd and managed to gain entry to the mosque. By stepping on the seated men's knees we edged our way to a corner of the balcony where we thought we saw a possible body space. There was literally no space in the entire mosque either to sit or stand. On that occasion I deeply wished to have been lowered by a sheet from the dome of the mosque to sit beside the pastor and to be at the heart of the drama.

By some quirk a space was made in our corner. As I crouched my elbows were pressed into my ribs by those around me and my knees were in my face. I knew that Mr. Kashani was behind me, but I dared not attempt to turn. I had never been in a Christian church under quite these circumstances, even at Easter. I felt as though I was stuffed into a railroad boxcar with a herd of humanity and no ventilation. The men about me seemed to pay no attention to me, for they were engrossed in the seriousness of the occasion. We were packed so close that it felt that we all were only heartbeats away.

The same evangelist was preaching, but now he intoned with much more emotion. As he approached the time of the Husain narrative, all lights were extinguished except for a spotlight on the pulpit area and the evangelist. I could see the pastor sitting very prominently at the first step, and I sighed with relief that my pale face wasn't spotlighted to a thousand Muslims or more in one of their most obedient moments.

The evangelist narrated the death of Husain's brother in the battle at Kerbala as the silence of the worshipers grew thicker. He described the severing of his brother's arms. Next, he depicted the death of Husain's sister's son. Husain had carried the young lad in his arms to the edge of the enemy lines to plead for water. The enemy took the child, killed him, and offered the dead body back to the mother. With every detail the moans and cries grew deeper and louder. Men began to slap their foreheads while others began beating their chests. Handkerchiefs were waved in the air and heads were bowed. Women screamed from their section of the balcony. There were constant chants of the name of Husain. "Oh Husain! Oh Husain! May I take your place."

After some twenty minutes of loud crying and beating of chests and swaying of heads the crowd calmed down as the narrative ended. At moments I admit I was a bit concerned. I was the only foreigner in a sea of emotional Muslims. My student friend was somewhere in the background. Peculiar thoughts crossed my throbbing brain as my body was nudged by elbows and hands and feet. What if I were the enemy, the threat, the intrusion on sacred ground! Had I not been challenged often by Muslims as an American whose government supported the Jews in Palestine against the Muslims? Had I not been suspected by some Muslim pastors and told to my face that I just might be a CIA agent? In the blur of ecstatic behavior what were my chances? Without difficulty I had been about to cry at the height of the narration of cruelty and tragedy. These Muslims were vicariously suffering with the drama of the Husain family. And I was suffering, too.

The lights were turned on and as tearful eyes became sober the evangelist led the people in prayers. He especially prayed for the Muslim brothers who were imprisoned and the people responded enthusiastically with the name of Husain. It took some time for the crowd to disperse and I was extremely pleased to be reunited with Mr. Kashani.

As we walked away from the crowds, Mr. Kashani informed me that many people were present in the mosque who had relatives in political prisons in Tehran. That was the reason why they called on Husain to help in freeing their loved ones from tyranny and injustice, in his words. I told him that they were very strong words. He replied that some of the best known religious leaders in the country had been silenced in their preaching through imprisonment or house arrest. I had heard that enough to begin believing it now. I felt a bit uncomfortable with the subject as we passed the crowds on the sidewalk, so I attempted to change the topic of conversation.

I told him that I was emotionally moved during the sermon and narration. I asked his impressions. "Do you recall the frequency of the use of the word, blood, especially the blood of Husain, by the evangelist?" he asked. I asked him to explain its usage. "The blood of Husain and his family is meritorious for all obedient Iranian Muslims. Husain knew what it meant to suffer under an evil and unjust rule. He is not only an example of righteous suffering in behalf of us Muslims, but we believe he is inspirational for the return of the last Imam to be our ruler and correct the wrongs of our times."

Then all the crying was out of despair and hope, I thought. Mr. Kashani was saying that out of felt oppression, the people yearned for a deliverer. What a potent force to be reckoned with if it were allowed to expand outside the mosque! Here were the possible seeds of revolution. I thought first, and then openly expressed to Mr. Kashani, "Jesus Christ was crucified, in part from political motivations, and his death reverberated throughout the world to confront political leaders and religious followers. And here in your world, you look to Husain as your martyr who can challenge those who are disobedient to him." Mr. Kashani responded, "That is right, but what can little people do?"

The next day was Ashura, the holiest day in the Iranian Muslim calendar. Mr. Kashani had promised to take me to the largest covered bazaar in the world, in south Tehran, and to one of the largest mosques in the city to hear his brother preach to some three thousand men about the death of Husain. I just didn't know if I was up to it. Had not the American Embassy advised all Americans in the city to remain off the streets that day? With such emotional displays in street parades and mosque gatherings, things might get out of hand, especially for a foreigner. But what had I grown my long shaggy beard for, but for such a day as this? Why, with a black coat and trousers, and a black hat, and a beard covering my pale American face, I just might pass for one of the crowd. And Mr. Kashani would be disappointed if I did not hear his brother preach from such a prestigious pulpit on such a sacred day. In fact, his brother had invited me to come and share the experience. I could hardly wait, although I too was tired from the fasting season, and the pilgrimage season, and now nearing the conclusion of the Muharram season.

As I prepared for sleep that night, a thousand thoughts raced through my mind. "Professor, how much obedience does Christianity take?" I imagined myself in a stateside seminary in a class taught by a visiting Muslim preacher. Could it really be reversed this way? What could you answer to his question of obedience? You could quote Scripture. You could share the personal knowledge of Jesus Christ which claims you. And these might be appropriate.

You might try to hook into his mentality and wave length. But how defensive and careless we often become when another religion questions us. "Well, let's see! We don't fast because its never been our habit; you see, we are really an affluent people and really don't have too many beggars. We pay taxes, and . . . could I buy you a Coke at the student store?"

Or maybe we say something like this. "We really don't make

pilgrimages to the Holy Land as a big thing in our religion. But on the other hand some do and more are doing it, as a sort of a prestigious thing, you know. In fact, here is a clipping from a religious magazine which says, 'Sign up now for your tour of the Holy Land—first rate accommodations, three square meals a day, air-conditioned buses to follow the footsteps of Jesus.' I even hear that there are several hundred thousand refugees in and around the Holy Land."

Or we blurt out these words, "In our religious experience the main time we cry is at funerals, and not many men cry at that. However, we take seriously the death of Jesus because he died on a cross for us. In fact I can show you a cross which I keep, keep, keep. . . ." Yes, a cross which is kept around the neck. Well, maybe it wouldn't go like this at all. Maybe, the Christian's obedience would be of such testy mettle that the Muslim preacher would gasp in awe, if not be troubled at his own obedience patterns. After all, have I not been the real loner in a world of Muslim obedience? Have I not been tested and at opportune times tested those about me?

It is late, and I must sleep some before the big day tomorrow. But this season of obedience still bothers me. Joan has been feeding me books on Nikos Kazantzakis, and some of his thoughts mesh with mine. How am I really obedient in the context which I feel I have been led into and have also freely chosen?

I believe that truth will change my life radically and my Muslim friends must become warm flesh. God has broken out of his house in heaven and Mecca, or any other symbol which we hold, and has put on sandals and is walking the streets. Not just a promise of a gift, but a gift given. Not an idea, or a ritual, or a religious practice, or a feeling—important as they all may be in our creaturehood. Jesus Christ passes by, and in my need, in the blind man's need, we all reach out. And the light of life and the bread of life is vital enough, transforming enough, to change me into a follower in obedience, and in that obedience I take the risk of relating to that Muslim in his home territory on God's good earth.

Why is sleep so fitful tonight? Does not the real generosity of the future lie in giving much to the present? I may save a lifetime for the pilgrimage to Jerusalem or to Mecca, and forfeit the moment of vibrant life that has been granted to me. Strategy and plans and futuristic ambitions might not be worth one thought and one step, unless this immediate present is filled until the cup overflows. Jesus, Jerusalem, the blind man . . . the cross might truly and deeply have been misunderstood if Jesus had passed the blind man by in his need. Perhaps I will be often surprised in the streets of Tehran by remembering the last judgment scene before the Christ. "When did I see you crying and lonely in the prison of your soul? When did I see you boneless and dehydrated? When did I see you tattered?" And the answer comes, "When you were in obedience giving refreshment of cup and spirit to the now person. Be with those who fast and take pilgrimages and mourn for a Savior, for I am with you there also."

Is not obedience returning to difficult places which have caused you undue hardships in this pilgrimage of obedience, where there may have been rejection, bypassing, the challenge of the very best within you? Leave, at least, for a time and space, those places of reward where you have had the greatest satisfaction, acceptance, or success. For surely those persons have a claim on you, as an obedient follower. They may not readily build up your ego, your prestige, your status, or your pride, but they need you as warm flesh, as one who walks in the spirit, as one who stands beside. Does not the blind man come to that street corner, year after year, to his place of failure, if you please, only to receive a few coins? But one day after all that returning, he received new eyes and a new life because warm flesh had passed by and the present was taken seriously as a matter of life and death, light and darkness.

Tomorrow is Ashura. Can the streets hold the flow of tears? I'll be ready by 7 A.M., for it is a long ride to the bazaar on a crowded day.

The next morning we set out for the bazaar at 8 A.M., attempting to hail a taxi, but there was no use. What taxis passed by us were filled to capacity with people sitting in each other's laps. We finally hailed a private car and headed south. Within six blocks of the bazaar we were stopped by the police who were allowing no cars to penetrate further. I could see why. The streets, even this far away from the main gates of the bazaar, were crowded with various groups of men and boys parading, chanting, and beating their chests with chains. Mosques and religious organizations throughout the city had gathered their males in the vicinities of the bazaar area to stage their religious marches. All of these activities were under the careful eyes of the police. Mr. Kashani explained that in former times men all over the country used to don white robes and march in honor of the martyrdom of Imam Husain. Many of the men would cut themselves with knives to draw blood which would stain their white garments to demonstrate their sharing in the martyrdom of the saint. But now all that had been surpressed by the authorities, except in a few remote villages. I could readily understand the possibilities of what that kind of emotionalism might do, fanned by oratory against either real or imagined enemies.

Even as we approached the narrow, winding alleyways within the bazaar, the marching men and boys were so thick that it was difficult to squeeze past them. I saw one group accompanied by drums, cymbals, and a cornet, as they beat their chests with both large and small chains, depending, I imagine, upon their size, or faithfulness, or their pain threshold. Black flags were carried by the marchers, as well as green banners inscribed with Qur'anic sayings. Up and down the alleyways there were huge containers of water, wrapped in black cloth. This water represented a gift by the bazaar merchants to tired, thirsty, deserving marchers, and offered a reminder that Imam Husain and his family were denied a simple cup of water in their battle and subsequent siege by the Sunni forces.

There are many mosques in the bazaar district, but on this day we were going to the mosque where Mr. Kashani's brother was to be the main speaker. The entry to the mosque was blocked by a mass of humanity. I noticed some ten flag poles leaning against the wall near the mosque gates. It was evident that some groups had ceased their marching and entered the mosque, though it didn't appear to me that the street scene had missed their presence. The question was how to gain entry into such a crowd.

Through the technique of push and shove, we wedged ourselves between man after man until we reached one of the many alcoves of the huge mosque. I estimated some three thousand men seated on the carpeted floor. Mr. Kashani explained that since 9 A.M. there had been four mullahs in succession who had ascended the pulpit and preached on the Husain theme. We could hear the fourth one over the public address but could not see him for we were still some distance from the pulpit. As this mullah concluded some of the men left and we rushed as best we could to a vantage point very near the pulpit. I had learned that in such activities one does not pause to say "Excuse me" for that would not be the Iranian thing to do. Besides, in the mosque as in the street, the one who gets a foot, head, or car bumper in front has the right of way by simple fulfillment of space.

It was near noon, now, and Mr. Kashani's brother mounted the twelve step mambar, covered with a green cloth on which were Arabic inscriptions of praise to Allah. A picture of the prophet hung from above. The crowd became hushed. The only sound came from the processionals outside. Mr. Mujtahedzadeh, a name his brother had assumed, dressed in a white turban, a black robe, and a green shiny ring began to speak softly over the still mass of men. He spoke of the goodness of the prophet, the wisdom of Ali, and the noble and brave heritage of the Shiite family. The only movement in the vast throng came from the tens of water bearers stepping over the carpet of men offering each a cup of water in the name of Husain. At 11:45 A.M., Mr. Mujtahedzadeh began chanting the narrative of Husain.

He referred to his cruel death at the hands of the Sunni forces, to the severing of his head, to his running blood. With great oratory and movement of head and hands, he excited the crowd into deep groans, loud cries, pounding of foreheads, and beating of chests. Exactly at noon he stopped the narrative and the mourning gradually subsided.

Then Mr. Mujtahedzadeh led the men in prayers for the sick, and for the Muslims to gain their rightful homeland and cherished holy places in Palestine. He descended the mambar, and to my utter amazement, came directly to me, shook my hand, and invited me to visit his home. With this gesture, he was off through the crowd as hundreds of men reached for his hand.

As we arrived once again in the alleyways of the bazaar the processionals were still in progress. I suggested that we go to a teahouse where we could have some chelo-kabab, for I wanted to treat Mr. Kashani for his hospitality to me during the past several days. I wanted to also find a retreat where we could not only eat but talk over the day's affairs.

As we ate our meal, Mr. Kashani told me of his brother. "This year my brother was given the privilege of speaking at noon at the mosque. Our traditions tell us that it was at noon that Imam Husain was near death and Allah gave him permission to die. My brother has been trained well as a mullah; he has known the right people, and for a man of forty years, he has progressed in the ranks very well. As you could probably tell, he is an excellent preacher. He makes good money all through the year as he preaches in mosques all over the country, and in homes that schedule him a year in advance. My brother cannot afford to say anything against the government because he has aspirations to climb the ladder of success. Any slip of the tongue would brand him as an untrusted mullah. Do you remember in the mosque last night when the preacher prayed for those in political prisons. My brother would never do such a thing."

I had realized all along that Mr. Kashani was a thinker of a different stripe than many of the students I had known. And now it was interesting to observe differences of opinion within the same family. "My brother," he continued, "plays safe. He says just enough for the common people to become emotional about the possibilities of their religion, but he refrains from saying too much, as many of our mullahs have done and ended up in trouble. So my brother is permitted to speak wherever he is invited, because he will not be critical of the establishment. So you see, there are two kinds of mullahs in our country, the safe kind and the silent kind. The safe kind are given a kind of freedom and the silent ones have been silenced because they took upon themselves too much freedom to speak the truth. It is sad that there is so much corruption."

The drama of the day still fascinated me. All the men, all the signs, all the marching, all the crying, all the giving of water! "What will these men do tomorrow?" I asked. "How will they settle down from such activity over the last ten days?" My student friend slowly sipped his tea and then laughed, "They will drown in their tears. It is all motion. It leads nowhere. In Iran we now have Bayer aspirin. It soothes for a while and then you need more. Today was good medicine. Tomorrow will be the same."

Well, I had lived through ninety days of religious fury. Black flags still flew for days afterwards, and hajjis told tales of their trek to Mecca. And blind men still stood on their street corners begging, while a blind mullah in his small way enacted a drama of world significance as he gave coins turned into food as a sacrifice during the fasting season. The way had been opened for me to enter the very heartland of the Muslim world. Perhaps it was as a stranger to the thousands I touched shoulders with in the intensity of their worship moments. Very few spoke to me, and maybe not many more noticed me, in spite of my fears of recognition in crucial moments of their devotion. Yet, I was there witnessing a drama of agony and ecstasy, of lost history, and future hope. And at times there was the opportunity to speak a word from my own world of knowledge and faith.

I know better than to think my presence was lost among the individuals or masses of people I rubbed elbows with. The Iranian is too curious to neglect such an idiosyncrasy in his midst. There would be hundreds of other homes and mosques to visit as word spread that someone was interested in them. And I knew better than to believe that their obedience season ended with Muharram. For the faithful whose families had been obedient to Islam for centuries there would be seasons of obedience every day. The lessons of the days had not been lost on me. And I hoped that I had caused a small ripple in that ocean of humanity.

7 God, King, and Country

The handsome, stern, and monarchial face confronts you in the shoeshop, the classroom, the visor of the taxi, the simple home, and on banners in the streets. It may be simply or exquisitely framed, but it is conspicuously present in every nook and cranny of every city and village and roadstop in Iran. I think confront is the right word. The picture makes you pause and wonder about this man, this more than man in presence; this nearest being to a god of authority and power on Persian soil. History tells us that he used to be taken lightly, not only in world circles, but among his own countrymen. He was a playboy of cars, planes, and women. At one time he was the powerless son of Reza Khan. His father was only a colonel in the Persian militia. But Reza Khan soon became Reza Shah the Great as he founded the Pahlavi dynasty, and he was called "King of Kings," "Shadow of the Almighty," "Vice Regent of God," and "Center of the Universe." And his son, Mohammed Reza Shah Pahlavi, was not to be denied his place of grandeur in the line of Pesian royalty. He was to grow into the role of Shahenshah, king of kings, and dream dreams of following King Cyrus into world renown.

I have never met the Shah. I have only seen him at a distance. But I have read his autobiography, his speeches, and heard his addresses on Iranian television. I have taught in the university founded by his father and one in which he has a great stake. I have also served on the faculty of a college in which he is a most benevolent patron. I taught English to the librarian of his royal library and I conversed with hundreds of his people who had much or very little to say about him. So I feel that I am familiar with this powerful monarch as much as a foreigner might know a king.

Let me simply refer to him as the Shah. He has been a dreamer all his life. This is one of the fascinating facets of his personality—his dreams. There are many more fascinating things to be said of him, of course, like his marriages to an Egyptian princess or to an Iranian tribal lady or to the commoner with no royal lineage of recent times, who finally furnished him with male heirs. But there is something peculiar about the great figures in Middle Eastern history. They dream dreams and act on them.

The Shah was to have visions and dreams in his early adolescence and early manhood that had deep significance for him. After all, his father had named him appropriately after two outstanding religious figures. Mohammed was the name of his prophet, and Reza was the name of the eighth Shiite Imam who was buried on Iranian soil. When the young Shah was Crown Prince and was being educated in Switzerland, away from family and homeland, he recalls that he faithfully said his prayers and read the Qur'an. In those years he secretly began to formulate plans to help his poverty-stricken countrymen. Once when he was bedridden with typhoid fever he dreamed that Imam Ali came to him with a bowl of liquid and told him "Drink." He regained his health. On another occasion when he fell from his horse he had a vision of Saint Abbas coming to his aid. He was not harmed in the fall. In difficult decisions he has had visions of the Twelfth Imam, his head circled by a halo, coming to him to give counsel and direction.

The Shah makes no bones about it. Allah is his friend and protector. He was saved from an airplane crash as he inspected an irrigation dam constructed for the benefit of the farmers of the country. He was led into battle and protected by Allah as he liberated

Azerbaijan from Russian control. He has survived several assassination attempts, some at point-blank range, because the hand of Allah intervened. His most critical experience was in the early fifties when Prime Minister Mossadeq nearly toppled him from his reign, but he believes that under the influence of Allah, he and the Iranian people were able to put Mossadeq and his forces down. From that moment on, the Shah was to lead his nation into its greatest days.

In my penetration into the Muslim world, I came to realize that I had tasted of the fruits of Islam at the grassroots in street corner mosques, in alleyway homes, and in the student world, as well as other places. I had picked up some disenchantment with the established political order. In fact, there was a feeling on the part of these people of a kind of competition between their religion and what they called a political religion. In American terms, it would be a churchly religion versus a civil religion. But I had not sought out persons involved in this so-called political religion. So I decided to spend time with the other side, that side which had been increasingly referred to as the Shah and his people. It was to prove to be a fascinating world and it served as a balancing experience for me. In fact, I believe it enabled me to not only appreciate both sides but also to allay the fears of some that I was one-sided in my interests and approach.

There was no doubt in my mind. By word and deed the Shah was a religious man and he cultivated a religious establishment around him. But it should be so. The modern Iranian constitution of 1906 had officially stated that Iran should be a Muslim Shiite Nation. The Shah had officially assumed the throne upon his father's abdication by placing his hand upon the holy Qur'an. His religious motivation and thinking was the stuff that dreams were made of. It only took his "White Revolution" of 1963, later named "The Revolution of the Shah and the People," to initiate his plan of redemption for his country. Its principles of land reform, worker's profit-sharing, houses of justice, educational and health and literacy corps, and many others appeared as a prophet's road map from Allah for establishing justice and righteousness in the land. In political speeches, in inaugurations of parliament sessions, in mass communications of radio and television, the Shah propagated that the blessings of Iran rested upon this kind of revolution. "By the grace of Almighty Allah" success would be given through the Shah's Revolution.

There it was! A plan of redemption! And the young king who had struggled for much of his political life for survival from the paws of the great powers had come into his own. He was on the way to becoming the prophet-king, the charismatic Imam, a savior of his people. And he had more, much more, than his religious dreams. He had the wealth of oil. And oil wealth translated into American jets, tanks, and guns meant that the prophet-king had a terrible swift sword in his hand. And he had much more than that. By the late sixties, he had developed with American help one of the most tightly knit, sophisticated, and effective domestic security forces in the world. The Twelfth Imam had returned in the form of the king, and the reign was on.

Is this some scenario from my fluid imagination? Have I drunk too deeply of the tea leaves? Let's move on into the world of the Shah's religion and meet the people and places which sound its calls.

In the heart of downtown Tehran is a building complex which houses the Religious Endowments Organization, known in Persian as Awqaf. A student friend had arranged an appointment for me with one of its officials. As I approached the entrance gate I noted that across the street was a cocktail lounge. This seemed rather ironic to me to have an alcoholic dispensary directly opposite the organization that administered the holy trusts of pious and faithful Muslims. But ironies abound all over Iran in this country come of age. Awqaf is actually administered by a deputy prime minister under the supervision of the Shah himself. As I awaited to see the official I thought of how formidable a bureaucracy this endowments organization had become. This was soon to be confirmed verbally as I was ushered into the official's office.

Mr. Ezzati was a balding man, chubby and short. He made me feel right at home because he came out from behind his imposing desk to greet me and to sit down on the divan. More often, Iranian bureaucrats will use the desk to show their authority or to maintain their aloofness from visitors by sitting behind it during the conversation. But not Mr. Ezzati. We were drinking tea instantaneously and chatting about his university training in the United States.

"Awqaf is the second richest institution in Iran, right behind the National Iranian Oil Company," he impressed upon me. "We possess an exceptionally large number of endowed properties which good religious people have deeded in trust to us. In some parts of the country, lands under various trusts make up about eighty percent of the total land available to the area. We operate on the assumption that all these properties under trust are meant to be used for the good of all people, not just for the trustees or the mullahs who are named to hold the deeds of trust."

I had gathered much earlier in my experience in Iran that Awqaf controlled the purse strings of much of the endowed lands which made it a very powerful organization. "What are the major responsibilities of Awqaf?" I asked Mr. Ezzati.

"Awqaf basically administers the affairs of all endowments in Iran. When a Muslim desires to leave money or land to a mosque or another religious organization, we aid him in the legal aspects and guarantee him that his trust shall be correctly used. We really supervise in one way or another all ecclesiastical affairs. But there are other responsibilities. We supervise the big enterprise of the pilgrimage to Mecca. We organize the caravans of people, schedule the jets, arrange the accommodations in Saudi Arabia, and safeguard the health of the travelers. That in itself is a big business. We administer the program which the Shah recently established which we call the Religious Corps. It is composed of the youth of our country who are trained in the Islamic sciences and who are sent out to the villages and cities to teach the people the principles of Islam. And then we promote our own Islamic culture with other countries around the world. You see, there is much work to be done in our organization."

Mr. Ezzati had said enough intriguing things to stimulate a barrel full of questions. I already knew that there were hostile feelings among the mullahs concerning this new Religious Corps. It was like the American president recruiting and training youth to send them out into the churches to set the people straight on their religion. Well, not quite! The mullahs were evidently threatened by it, which seemed natural to me. I wanted Mr. Ezzati to say more about this program so I innocently asked, "When you have so many mullahs and mosques in the country, why do you feel it necessary to train and send out these youth? You have religious schools and seminaries to do this job, don't you?"

He had anticipated my question and launched into an explanation. He said that mullahs had always presented problems to Awqaf. They consider themselves as owners of endowed properties and misuse them for their own purposes. Awqaf distrusts mullahs in the administration of finances and properties, and consequently Awqaf must control all these matters. He explained that his organization was training a new mullah type in the Religious Corps. The Shah in 1970 had ordered the formation of a new corps of youth, similar to the existing literacy and health corps. The youth were to be trained in religion and sent out across the country to lead the people in their religious orders.

"Our young men used to go to schools to become mullahs in order to avoid the national draft service. Now the Shah has ordered that these young men serve in the Religious Corps and has assigned Awqaf the responsibility of training them. In the past at the age of seven, students entered these religious schools and wore the dress of a mullah. Really, a little boy wore a turban and cloak. When we learned that some twelve thousand students like this were studying in hundreds of religious schools, we issued regulations that a student should be fifteen years old before entering such a school. At the present time about three thousand religious corpsmen have been recruited from these schools. We have trained them and sent them out to teach the holy Qur'an, the White Revolution principles, endowment affairs, and many other matters. I must be truthful to say that their work is slow. At first the villagers are suspicious of them, like they are of any strangers. But when they realize these youth have been trained in the Islamic sciences, they will give their respect to them. Our biggest problem is the mullah who talks against the youth."

Mr. Ezzati had been gracious to allow me this visit in the busy season of the pilgrimage. He had confirmed one of my growing assumptions about the conditions of Islam in Iran. There were mutual suspicions and distrust between the grassroots Muslims and the official bureaucracy of the king and his religious associations. I had been surprised, however, at the candor with which Mr. Ezzati spoke. With reams of booklets and pamphlets in my attache case, Mr. Ezzati saw me to the door, for he had to run to the airport to see off another jet of pilgrims to Mecca.

As I walked out of the main gate and faced the cocktail lounge, my thoughts flashed to the Meshed Hyatt Hotel, a new hotel in the holy city of Meshed where pilgrims by the thousands flock each year to pay homage to Imam Reza, the eighth Shiite saint. Several years before I had spent a summer with my family in that eastern frontier city studying the Persian language. That was the first place in Iran where my wife felt the necessity to wear a chador in the public streets. The men of Meshed ceased to stare holes through her once she donned the chador. And that was the city where every morning at sunrise we were awakened by the hundreds of mullah voices from the minarets calling the faithful to prayer. The Imam Reza shrine was domed in brilliant gold which blinded one's eyes on the scorching summer days. Once we got permission to walk in the several courtyards of the shrine, but because we were non-Muslims we could not approach the tomb itself. The shrine was under the auspices of Awqaf.

Since those days, Awqaf had used monies from the shrine endowments in the building of the Meshed Hyatt Hotel, a luxury hotel in every dimension, serving the best cuisine and alcoholic beverages that American and European exporters could offer. Nothing could irritate mullahs more than to take away their rights to administer endowments, except maybe to use those holy monies and properties to serve up what they consider the devil's offerings. I recalled from newspaper accounts how the mother of the queen had officially opened the seven million dollar hotel whose "original investment was made by the Holy Shrine of the Imam Reza Endowment Fund." After the opening, her official party made an official pilgrimage to the shrine. The shrine had become a gigantic and modern business under governmental direction.

I also remembered another newspaper account of Crown Prince Reza's visit to the shrine. The Shah and his family make annual pilgrimages to Meshed, and sometimes more often. Crown Prince Reza made a pilgrimage to the shrine one time only four days after an alleged plot against the Shah, the Empress, and the Crown Prince. The news caption ran something like this, "Crown Prince Reza's presence in the holy city provided an occasion for thousands of people to gather at the holy shrine to pray for the good health of the Shahenshah and members of the royal family." As I returned home and read some of the materials from Awqaf, I realized that both my own speculations and the "gut-level" feelings of many of the Muslims I had talked with were correct, at least in the fact that the Shah had gathered around himself a huge apparatus for an effective religious propagation.

But the religious endowments organization was only the beginning of the vast network of what I was beginning to see as the civil religion of Iran. I learned that the Shah Mosque in the heart of the Tehran bazaar was presided over by a mullah directly appointed by the Shah. In fact, the mullah was a relative of the late Prime Minister Mossadeq who had opposed the Shah. But this mullah stood by the Shah in his time of crisis with Mossadeq and served for a time as prime minister when the young Shah sought security for his rule. Later, the Shah was to appoint this mullah to preside over the activities and endowments of this huge mosque. He became the Shah's number one preacher and went with him on his pilgrimage to Mecca and prayed for him on every official occasion. It reminded me of the role that Billy Graham plays with some United States presidents, although this mullah's position is much more official and formal. Whenever the Shah Mosque, the King's Mosque, was brought up in conversations with other mullahs they ridiculed it.

Several of my student friends at the Royal Seminary and Mosque had told me of their duties in promoting the Shah's religion. The Royal Seminary and Mosque was located in the heart of a government complex of buildings, including the Parliament, the Plan Organization, and several other ministries. My student friend, Husain, a name literally given to tens of thousands of Iranian infants, was a mullah in training at this seminary under royal patronage. He had enrolled at the seminary in anticipation of becoming affiliated with some Iranian consulate abroad as its Islamic specialist, and as he told me, to escape the military draft. He said that some of the most noted educational and political leaders of modern Iran had attended this seminary, including the present speaker of the parliament.

One day Husain described a fascinating duty which he and his seminarian friends enacted. "Each day ten of us go by bus to Rey, a small town just outside the city where the Imamzadeh Abdol Azim and the tomb of Reza Shah the Great are located."

I had been there too, as a tourist, and had seen both buildings. I knew that the Imamzadeh was a shrine to a Shiite saint and that it was covered in a gold-plated dome. But I had to look at it from a distance, for only Muslims were permitted inside the tomb room. There was no problem to go inside the Reza Shah Shrine and pass around the mausoleum. "Who was Abdol Azim?" I asked Husain.

"Abdol Azim was the great teacher of our Imams and is one of the most respected saints in our religion. It is a place where many pilgrims go to make requests to the saint. But every week we go to the tomb of Reza Shah the Great to read passages from the Qur'an and to offer prayers to Allah in praise of him. One time as we were at the side of the tomb performing our duties, the Shahenshah entered, and the soldiers started to force us to leave. But the Shahenshah came over and ordered them to release us. Then he asked us to continue our readings and listened. When we had finished, he congratulated us and told us we had performed a great duty for our country. Since that day, every time we go to the tomb, the soldiers treat us with great respect."

What a gem of information! Here was a young seminarian telling me something about the very foundations of what I called the civil religion of Iran. I had known that the Shah had brought back the body of his father who had died in exile in South Africa and had placed it in the present tomb. I had also read that he added the title, "the Great," to his father's name. But two other bits of information were now put together. The Shah had built his father's tomb right beside one of the most cherished saints of the Shiite religion. When hundreds of thousands of the faithful came to make vows and gain merits at the saint's tomb, they would pass right by the father's tomb. The pilgrimage to the father's tomb would hopefully become just as important as the one to the saint's resting place. And secondly, young seminarians from his patronized school were sent out, not to the saint's tomb where the faithful had gone for centuries, but to the father's tomb to bless it in the name of Allah. Wasn't this a planned effort to bolster the prophet-king's religion?

But there was more news from Husain who was evidently becoming a product of the White Revolution and certainly a new mullah type in modern Iran. He told me what he and the seminarians did on the night of Ashura, the night before his namesake was killed in the battle at Kerbala.

"On the night of Ashura many high officials of the government and the Shah's court gather at the mosque at our school to observe the high mourning season. Some of the high ranking mullahs recite parts of the story of Saint Husain's martyrdom. Other mullahs offer prayers in memory of Husain and the other Imams, and at the same time, they include in their prayers the names of the Shahenshah, the Shahbanou (Empress), the Crown Prince, and Reza Shah the Great. We don't have to attend, but we are paid two hundred rials (about three dollars) if we do, and most of us go to stand with the crowd. Two hundred rials means a great deal to us."

Husain was indeed a propagandist for the religion built around the king of kings. If Awqaf and the Shah Mosque were not enough to persuade me that there was something to a double expression of religion in Iran, then the conversation with this seminarian of the Royal Seminary was proof of the pudding. It was for real. How real? Among the royalty, the bureaucrats, the elite, the government, it was solidly expressed. The Shahenshah sought not only the political loyalties of his people, but consciously planned to gain their religious affections. How real was it for the common folk? Well, for the mullahs and their followers and the student world of university and college, it was questionable. But for the illiterates who still make up most of the Iranian population, who still look for savior types to bring them salvation in this world as well as the next, there are possibilities.

On one occasion as I was leaving the Royal Seminary, a beggar woman standing in front of the mosque told me, "I go to the mosque every day to pray for the Shahenshah." I later learned that once upon a time the Shah had passed through her village and she had touched his hand and promised to pray for him every day. Well, she had a place on royal turf.

And what about Husain? He had dreams in his eyes of Allah, Shahenshah, and faraway places. He figured that he was in the most opportune place he could be. With a little luck (Enshallah—If Allah wills) and the Shah's continued patronage of him and the school, he just might become somebody in Iran. He would even be willing to abandon his turban and robe to go to America or become a high minister.

Through my teaching at the Faculty of Islamic Theology, which also was a government sponsored school, I had been introduced to many facets of the civil religion. Most importantly, I witnessed the great fleeing of the conservative mullahs from the faculty to other seminaries in Tehran and Qum and other religious schools. Through friends of the faculty I was introduced to the director of the Royal Library, Dr. Faez. Dr. Faez had been a star pupil at the Royal Seminary in his early student days. He had caught the eye of Reza Shah the Great, and the Pahlavi King had named him to be the dean of the embryo Faculty of Islamic Theology of the University of Tehran. He had served in that capacity for some twenty-five years and had retired with distinction. But the present Shah would not let him rest and named him to head up the Royal Library at the Golestan Palace. Dr. Faez spoke fluent Arabic and French, but in his older age he desired to become more fluent in English, since several of his children were studying and living in the United States. Thus, he had heard of the American professor at the faculty who taught English and Comparative Religions.

My first visit to the library was memorable, as were all my other journeys into its little world. The library was housed within the tract of land and gates and palace known as the Golestan. Presidents, potentates, and kings of various nations had been housed within the palace proper, including Queen Elizabeth and President Nixon. Tourists were allowed to see the grounds and the ballroom of the palace at selected times. The high gates were guarded by the red-capped Iranian militia. The only automobiles allowed within the gates were those of officials, usually in Mercedez-Benzes.

On the Saturday morning which Dr. Faez scheduled for me to come to his office to converse with him in English, I set out in the heavy traffic in my small, Iranian-built, four cylinder Peykon car. My students at the Faculty of Theology had long teased me over my little yellow car. They thought all Americans living in Tehran were aristocrats, including professors. After all, wasn't it quite expensive to fly one's family across thousands of miles and live in such an expensive city as Tehran? And if taxi drivers could afford Mercedez-Benzes to haul around pedestrians who couldn't even afford a donkey, shouldn't their esteemed professor drive something better than the "cheap and inferior" Peykon? I had long decided that it was better for life, limb, and sanity to stay clear of taxis and personal cars in the city streets, but there were times when distances were too far to walk or taxis were impossible to find. So on this morning I set off to see this distinguished man.

Dr. Faez had failed to leave word with the gate guards that I was to be admitted, both myself and the yellow Peykon. I found this out as I drove up to the gate. I was halted by bayoneted guards and asked my business. I persuaded them to telephone Dr. Faez, as they insisted that I park the Peykon on the parking spaces adjacent to the entrance. I didn't mind following their advice, especially as their weapons were larger than mine. But then, a car in the hands of an Iranian driver is a formidable weapon. From their conversation with Dr. Faez they were assured that I was bona fide in these non-visiting hours, but the car was another thing. They were adamant that I park it outside.

I had learned a few things about communication in the Iranian milieu. I left the engine running, jumped out of the car in a dramatized fit of rage, and rushed to the phone in the guard booth shouting that I would telephone Dr. Faez. Either they were overcome by this foreigner playing the part of an Iranian, or they were worried that another telephone call to the doctor might get them in hot water. They quickly opened the dual iron gates and I sped my little car in and placed it beside an official Mecedez-Benz, not fifty yards from the entrance to the library.

The doorman whisked me into the most ornamental office I had ever been in. Mirrored glass over the walls! French provincial furniture! A larger than life, beautifully framed picture of the Shahenshah! And Persian carpeted floor so thick it was like walking on air! But what I remember most was a Carolina blue telephone on a mammoth oversized desk. My children were such University of North Carolina fans that I wished they could have seen it. It did seem so incongruous with its surroundings.

Dr. Faez in a dark black suit, short in stature with a goatee of gray short whiskers, came to me and took my hand. He must have been seventy years old. He led me to the divan where a hot pitcher of tea and sweets were awaiting. In his broken English we conversed about his life. He was born in Meshed where his father was a famous mullah. He had studied in the religious schools, and he had memorized the Qur'an at his father's feet. He had studied in Europe and had come back to teach literature in the new university founded by Reza Shah. When the Shah selected him to head the Faculty of Theology, he willingly gave his life to it for some twenty-five years. And he continued to serve Mohammed Reza Shah Pahlavi, even into his retirement, in the Royal Library.

Of course, my main task was to help him practice his English. I always found it difficult to correct his pronunciation and reading, but he was a good-natured old man and he was always a willing learner. Among the many subjects of our conversations, we talked about the Faculty of Theology.

He used to say, "Reza Shah's greatest ambition was to modernize Iran. And he felt that he must modernize the mullahs if Iran was to make progress. He wanted me to introduce modern subjects into the curriculum of the faculty and to train the mullahs in the new sciences and law. His command was a difficult one, and after over two decades I still was not successful."

"Why was it so difficult?" I asked him. With practically every serious question I asked him, he would stroke his goatee and pause and speak very deliberately.

"My assignment was to change a traditional mullah into a modern one. Reza Shah felt that the superstitions and corruption in our religion would hinder progress. He made it very difficult for the religious leadership in our country to continue to work from their traditional positions of power and fame. He closed the religious schools. He placed the endowments under the government's control. He established civil courts to replace the religious courts presided over by the mullahs. He actually began to break their backs."

In my teaching in the faculty I had noticed a decline in the mullahs who wore the traditional mullah garb each year. I asked him about that trend.

"It has been occurring for many years. More of our young people have entered the universities and colleges and trade schools to prepare for better vocations in the new Iran. And the young men who wanted to be mullahs like their fathers have enrolled in the religious schools which were still open to them. In the Faculty of Theology today most of the men are trained to teach Islamic subjects and other knowledge in our schools operated by the government. The teacher in suit and tie is becoming much more prominent than the mullah in turban and robe."

Although it was always a ticklish question to which most Iranians responded in an evasive manner, or responded not at all, I asked him, "What has been your experience under the Shahenshah?"

"Our Shahenshah is a very religious man with a strong mind and a powerful will. He respects our religion deeply. I have seen it so, for I have been with him at his invitation on the pilgrimage to Mecca. He desires more than anything that our people learn the true values of our religious heritage and practice them in sound principles. History will show him to be one of our greatest kings."

I always felt that Dr. Faez wanted to say more to the questions that I asked him, for he was a man of great intellect and worldwide vision. He had studied comparative religions. He always spoke highly of Zoroastrianism, Christianity, and Judaism. Once he told me, "I respect you as a Christian, and I make it a practice to study Christian literature. I wish that we Muslims could exemplify more of the ethics of love found in your Bible."

Our conversations in English continued, and I parked my little car within the gated walls each Saturday as the soldiers nodded their heads at my passing. Dr. Faez confirmed what I had already seen and heard. The ominous picture of the Shahenshah did confront you, often in strange and mysterious ways across the country. And there was another confrontation. The Shahenshah was continually tooling and retooling his religious and political ideas and institutions to make his own brand of religion a fait accompli.

The reality of the Shah's religion came home to me audibly in several ways. There was a military training camp located within shouting distance of my house in Tehran. Often, my boys and I would walk the sand dunes near the barbed wire fence which surrounded the camp. The young soldiers as they marched would shout, "Khoda, Shah, Mihan," interpreted "God, King, and Fatherland." Or across the wall to which my window at the college opened, I could hear the young voices of elementary school children as they stood erect in the school courtyard and shouted as they began the day's activities, "God, King, and Fatherland." Surely the young soldiers and children were being socialized into the beliefs and values of a prophet-king.

But what did all of this Awqaf, Shah Mosque, Royal Seminary, Imam Reza Shrine, the Tomb of Reza Shah the Great, Faculty of Theology, and a thousand other sights and sounds of like kind have to do with the way I taught or related to people? I think the meaning of it all is seen in the call of the minaret. I have a number of color slides of this slender, tall, spiraling arm of the mosque which twirls its way to the skies, far above the dome of the mosque, the village or city streets, as it reaches out for the heavens. For centuries the mullahs have ascended the narrow steps within the minaret to arrive at the top and shout, or better chant, loudly in Arabic, the words which alert the people that it is time for prayer. In more recent times, electronics have taken over this function, and in many minarets, a prerecorded tape sounds the call to prayer by the mullah. Through the years the mullah has called the people to prayer, has taught them the Qur'an, has preached from the pulpit, has directed the religious schools, and has served in the interim time of the Imams until the Twelfth Imam's return. In religion the mullah has been kingpin.

But no more! The Shah has issued his own call of the minaret. He has welcomed the ordeal of putting the mullah in his place, of modernizing his country from the simple, superstitious ways of the remote village to the mechanized, chaotic ways of the city. His religious aides control the monies of the faithful through the endowments. His educational specialists inculcate the younger generation with the civil religion. His young mullah types in their sparkling new uniforms are sent out to the people with the message of salvation of the "White Revolution." And he has the power to back up his dreams of a "bloodless" revolution.

All of this means that there is a competition between the traditional forces of religion and the Shah's forces for loyalties, monies, peoples, and organizations. But I believe the battle is becoming rather one-sided, for the Shah holds most of the strings that determine the content of the call to prayer. He can close the doors of the mosque and collapse even the twelve step pulpit, and can muzzle if not silence the mullahs. All radio, television, newspapers, and publications are under the censorship of the government. The modern religious establishment has near complete control over the traditional one.

Nowhere in my experience in Iran did I see anything comparable to the happenings in the mid-sixties when traditional religious leaders barked louder when they felt their religious domains were threatened. In those days one of the leading mullahs of the holy city of Qum led a revolt over the question of women's rights to vote which had been launched as a reform movement by the parliament. It is reported that he said to the Shah, "It is not you who decides what is right; it is I and the other mullahs." That is the time when many of the mullahs' followers in Qum and Tehran lost their lives in bloody battles with governmental forces.

I am glad that it was my good fortune to mix, see, hear, and feel with all the religious elements in Iran. I never took sides in the struggle over the call of the minaret, though at times I knew I was being asked to do so. On one occasion a group of students who felt that their wages as teachers were unjust asked me to represent them at the government's office of education. I was not a lawyer, nor a lobbyist, and most especially I was not an Iranian who had any business in the affair. I was a guest of the Iranian people, and I intended to remain in the good graces of my visa. On too many occasions I heard criticism of the powers that be that were too strong and negative for me to repeat, but I did not agitate or urge those expressions.

The Irony of my situation was two-fold. My Americanness recalled to many Iranians the hopes of democracy, freedom, and liberty. They had tasted very little of these fruits. And yet, the Shah on many occasions had said that he welcomed the ordeal of "Westernization" and that it was wise to place as little restraint as possible upon ordinary citizens. Once he said, "To allow people to speak their minds not only provides a cathartic; it may also serve to uncover abuses." I was a representative of a country whose ideals inspired the dreams and aspirations of Iranians, including their king. Yet, America was looked upon as the provider of those things which provided coercive power to suppress those ideals which Iranians longed for. Repeatedly I was informed that America put down Prime Minister Mossadeq and preserved the rule of the Shah. Time and time again I was accosted by the account of America training the security forces of the Shah to reign tightly over the population. Often I was reminded that American business made their millions off Iranian oil and paid them pennies for it. And Vietnam! Students would ridicule before me the giant slayer of America and the paper tiger of a poor, underdeveloped people.

On the other hand my Americanness called attention to some that America was a Christian nation founded upon religious freedom. This they yearned for. Why could not the mullah speak from his pulpit? Why could not the mosque handle its own affairs? Why could not the people express their devotion to Husain and the other saints in their own ways? Of course I was reminded too often of the Christian Crusades that slaughtered Muslims in the Middle East, in the Holy Land. Even Dr. Faez called my attention to the love ethic in the Gospels which Iranians would do well to emulate, as well as American Christians to follow.

But there was a deeper irony in the country itself. For Islam was not a religion which said to render unto Caesar the things that are Caesar's and unto God the things that are God's. Islam was a complete religion in the sense that it provided a road map religiously, politically, economically, and socially for all Muslims. But more than that, Iranian Shiite Islam held the belief in an Imam or saint or prophet-king, call him what you will, who would return to earth to preside over a land filled with justice and righteousness. Given this road map with various interpretations by many aspiring religious leaders of the symbols, values, and practices of the religion, and Islam really served as a means of conflict and struggle for power and prestige between mullahs, kings, and others.

The irony is that in Iran, Islam has become split into two main camps. The Shah aspires to be prophet-king. The mullah attempts to act in behalf of the Twelfth Imam. The Shah enlightens the people with his "Bible," the "White Revolution," while the mullah quotes from the Qur'an. The Shah presides over a great complex of endowments, shrines, schools, universities, and colleges which promote his brand of Islamic religion, and the mullahs speak where they can from the thousands of mosques and smaller shrines which dot the landscape like the stars dot the heavens. And each is a competitor, each is threatened by the other, and each wants to be victorious.

And so ambivalences abound. Hide and seek games are played. Force is used, and life is lived in much tension. The question I always had to raise in my mind was, "How much of a risk is it to go where the people are?" One of the very first conversations I had with a mullah resulted in his counseling me to stay away from mosques because the people would consider me unclean as a non-Muslim and would embarrass me upon my entry into their holy ground. He was proved to be erroneous as I went into mosques throughout the country. I later heard that he was on the side of civil religion. On the other hand, I was advised by many mullahs that if I visited government agencies they would not give me any information. And yet I found warm and interested people in those places who were willing to discuss matters of religion with me. And so I had to decide upon the risks, and there were some.

There was one outstanding mosque and lecture hall which I had contacted through several friends. I had begun attending some of their programs. Their emphasis was revivalistic, a return to an enlightened Islam, appealing particularly to high school and college age youth. Both men and women in great numbers participated in small group meetings as well as mass gatherings. Evangelistic types both lectured and preached in the lecture hall. My plan was to become, as best a foreigner could, involved in the ongoing life of the mosque, to study their ways of religious life, and to meaningfully share through my relationships my own religious pilgrimage. That was not to be. Very abruptly while I was on leave in the United

States, the mosque was closed by the police and several of its leaders were put under house arrest. I learned about it when I returned.

A well-placed Iranian put it this way. "The security police closed the mosque down. One of the main leaders of the mosque was trained in France, especially in French Marxism. He saw Mohammed not so much as a sanctified prophet, but as a revolutionary, and Islam not as a religion per se, but as a revolutionary movement. He got into trouble with our Islamic conservative leadership by saying that Ali's father was a polytheist. The conservative mullahs were against him and the mosque. The government became wise to him when Marxist influences outside Iran criticized him on his erroneous blending of Marxist thought with Islam. The police arrested and detained the director of the mosque for three days and nights without food and water until he signed over the entire mosque properties to Awqaf. The police put the French-trained leader of whom I have spoken under house arrest, and to this day the mosque has remained closed."

In hindsight, if I had been a frequent participant in the mosque activities in its heyday, when it was closed I might have risked my good standing within both the modern and conservative camps of religious expressions. However, there is always a risk in a country like Iran where the main religion, Islam, claims to varying degrees the allegiance of some 98 percent of the people, and it is not only a religion but a political science. It deals with power and all its consequences. It deals with leaders who rise and fall. And especially Iranian Shiite Islam is founded and seemingly flourishes on tragedy, on vicarious suffering, on a lost hope.

My going into the civil religion world uncovered one truth which I forcefully affirm for my own understanding. The Shah, even within the bounds of his authoritarianism and near total power, has begun a revival of interests into things that are Persian, into the variety of peoples and communities which in spite of all their differences make up the Iranian nation. He deeply appreciates the Zoroastrians and their high moral values. I once heard the representative of the Zoroastrian community to the parliament refer in a speech to the invitation of the Shah for all Zoroastrians to return and live in freedom in their mother country. The Zoroastrians, a very small minority, yet a powerful influence in the lifeways of all Iranians, deeply appreciate the Shah and his protection of their rights in a monolithically Muslim nation.

And the Jews have been a prospering minority since King Cyrus freed them from the Babylonian captivity and gave them a homeland in Persia. They, too, would be among the first to sing the praises of the Shah in the granting to them of their religious liberties. The Shah has had special interest in Israel over the years and has attempted to live with both his "Arab Muslim brothers" and the Israelis over the issue of Palestine. An Israeli consulate has been steadily maintained in Iran when often Iran had severed her relations with Egypt or Iraq.

Not only Zoroastrians and Jews have felt the benevolent hand of the Shah, but also the Christian communities have basked in their freedom of religious expression. Both churches of the ancient sees of the Assyrians and the Armenians as well as those of more recent Roman Catholics, Protestants, and Anglicans dot certain portions of the country. These Christian communities are allowed representatives to the parliament also, just as the Zoroastrians and the Jews. The rumor circulated around circles with which I was acquainted that the Shah's sister had converted to Roman Catholicism and had a private chapel built in her palace. Missionaries from Christian churches in Europe and America have been allowed into Iran for centuries and have built hospitals, schools, book stores, and orphanages.

In some of the older Christian churches there is a restlessness. The Assyrian churches still speak Syriac in their homes and church services. They long for a land of their own in old Mesopotamia and still speak of their nationalistic aspirations. The Armenians have never forgotten the brutality shown them by the Turks and the loss of their homeland. So they write and speak and pray in their own language in their homes, schools, and churches, for a national homeland and remember their kinsmen in Soviet Armenia.

In the recent celebrations of the 2,500-year-ago founding of the nation under the great monarch King Cyrus all the religious minorities were quite vocal in their praise of the present Shah and their linking of him with King Cyrus in benevolences to them.

One of the new avenues which passed near my home was named after Dr. Jordan who established a famous boy's high school under the auspices of the Presbyterian mission to Iran. This naming could not have happened without the knowledge of the Shah.

Thus, just as there are ambivalences within all the religious expressions in Iran toward the Shah and toward each other, there is an ambivalence within me. But that is the ultimate risk one takes when one sojourns in a foreign and strange land. The land in time loses its foreignness, and the strangeness wears off, and the men and women, boys and girls, the high and the low, become human beings who cry, who struggle, who lord over others, who rejoice, who dream, who hope, who suffer, and who die. And when one leaves the relative safety of his home or office or friend's house he plunges into the mazeway of the mystery of life and becomes identified with it. I like God, Shah, and country. I like mullah, student, director, librarian, seminarian, the blind man, and the water server. In a time and a place there just may come a harmony to it all. I'm glad I was there with it all.

8 And the Beat Goes On

Growth! Expansion! Development! Progress! Destiny! One may find negative words in the streets and in hidden corners where bare feet hit the pavement and distressed souls confess their grievances. But in the newspapers, radio, and television which signal the official word, there is one sound. Iran will be the West Germany of both Europe and Asia within twenty years, so forecast the Shah and his coterie of technocrats. Another dream from the dreamer! Be careful! Oil money speaks powerfully from the second richest oil producer among the developing nations.

Already jumbo jets have upped the foreign population in Iran by thousands, including twenty thousand Americans. Some fifty thousand Americans alone are expected to jam the country by 1980. The great famine in Iran is the lack of managerial talent and skilled technicians to bring Iran into the age of modern technology. So foreigners multiply in Iran faster than the natives, and the pains of expansion bring the tumult of chaos. Rental houses for foreigners increase three hundred percent overnight. Elite schools based on English curriculum become overcrowded in days and compound the American drug and generation gap problems on foreign soil. Streets, already crowded with wheels and feet, stretch to the jubes (gutters) with added traffic and congestion.

The airport, long considered a place to forcefully abide time on checkout and check in, has become more hectic, especially as American companies fly jets full of families to settle in Iran to do the modernizing job. And the ports on the Persian Gulf have become nearly paralyzed as cargo ships await months to unload the "goodies" from the West which the oil money has purchased. And the beat goes on.

Christian churches are booming, especially for foreigners. Just recently, a Southern Baptist church was founded for English-speaking people and now accommodates over two hundred worshipers in its service. Iranian businessmen are filling their pockets with green dollars to such an extent that the Shah, personally, has vowed a battle against their corruption and has promised prison to those who are caught. American businesses run shuttle services to Iran to beg for lucrative contracts to build any and everything which will give the country the best of the material culture of the West. And Americans dream dreams of the wealth which will be theirs as they sign two-year contracts to live and work in Iran.

And culture shock! It works both ways. Iran is not yet American and will never be. The walls that surround every house and apartment and building! The crazy and death instinct traffic patterns! The only bowling alley! The expensiveness of everything! And a million other things cause the American's initial dreams of grandeur to sour, to become bitter, and to turn to plans of escape. And the beat goes on.

Some American families simply cannot cut it culturally; the bathroom stinks, the jube stinks, and the country stinks. Others see that the green money stateside quickly fades into the rust color of pennies, and they simply cannot or are not willing to hack it financially. They return to the states often disillusioned and cynical of the whole overseas experience. The American military's presence in Iran is not a bad post. Iran is not at war with anyone, at least outside the country. I believe the frustration for the American military advisors is the slowness of Iranians to learn the sophisticated ways of flying and maintaining ultramodern jet fighters, helicopters, and tanks. Iran seems to have an abundance of material, much of it rusting in the docks and in the deserts, and a woeful lack of trained or capable personnel to man the equipment.

There is another beat to some of the American and Westerner's intent to remain in the country. There are foreign men and women who devote time to learn the language and the cultural ways of the people. They belong to organizations which give benevolences to hospitals, orphanages, and struggling educational institutions. They are affiliated with churches which have the best interests of Iranians at heart in their outreach. I personally have seen numerous deeds of kindness—giving shelter to a homeless boy for months, employing a maid with good pay and taking on the upkeep of her down-and-out family, providing food and money to the perennial beggar who comes knocking on the iron gate, and making donations to every worthy Iranian cause.

Culture shock also affects Iranians. Why do without the big American car which you may purchase from a departing sergeant when you know it will be ill at ease on the streets of four-wheelers, small cars, and sheep? Why not buy the multi-channel color television set for triple its value from the Westerner eager to take that money and invest it in carpets, when in Iran there is just one channel and no color at all? Iranian style McDonalds, Pepsis, Bonanzas and Putt Putts! Discotheques with wild music and wilder dress shipped from abroad! A mushroom of English institutes for learning English to rival the hundreds of cinemas showing Western movies dubbed into the Persian language! And the Shah lecturing America on its corrupted greatness while at the same time stockpiling American weapons and goods which may very well corrupt his own people. Perhaps the greatest cultural shock comes both to the Iranian thinker and to the street pedestrian when he sees the free-thinking American, the free-spending American, the material-laden American, and when he thinks or dreams or says, "Why can't that kind of life be mine!" In his culture shock the American may flee back home to the shores of "liberty and plenty." The Iranian in his shock once again hides behind his walls, or walks the same streets a little more crowded with cars and pedestrians each day, or pours into the cinemas to vicariously live with thoughts and places not quite his own.

Indeed, the tempo in the country has picked up considerably. And where it will lead no one really knows. As long as the oil money holds out, foreigners will continue to come, and their life-styles will naturally affect Iranians. As a simple, illiterate, and heart-feeling servant said to me, "We hear on the radio and the television and the newspapers how much good our noble oil is doing our country. But I have to stand in longer lines for meat, bread, and rice. And sugar sometimes is not available. My children have to pay more tuition for their schooling, and my wages have not increased. And yet I see prosperity all around me."

Beneath the lights, glamour, prestige, and pride of Iranian purchased jumbo jets, F-14 fighter jets, hovercraft, proposed nuclear plants, steel mills, and the world's largest refinery, a different beat goes on. In fact, there are several beats all at once. The official beat is the sound of optimistic progress with no sour notes. From its perspective all things can be achieved if Iran follows the course plotted by its Shahenshah who desires to return the Persian nation to its worldwide glory and fame once experienced under the great King Cyrus. But only he really has the road map and the proper interpretation and means of power to accomplish its restoration. It is built on absolute monarchy.

Another strange beat goes on. It is the beat of discontent, and it is expressed in various ways. Recently, several American military personnel were murdered by dissident factions. Iranian police have been killed, bombs have exploded, and assassinations have been attempted. Seemingly, this is not widespread, but the firing squad is constantly revved up to deal with such violence.

More widespread discontent comes from those who consider themselves faithful to the true religion. In particular, there are many who eagerly anticipate the return of their Twelfth Imam, the Mehdi. The Mehdi is expected to right the wrongs, soothe the hearts of the poor and outcasts, and establish a just and righteous rule in the land. I have attended several of these "Twelfth Imam meetings," and the rumor I heard was that there are ninety of these meetings held regularly in Tehran alone. Men gather in private homes to pray for the return of the Twelfth Imam as they voice their condition of oppression and express their hope for change with the anticipated return of their prophet.

But more deeply, the discontent comes from the populace at large in the religious gatherings in the mosques, shrines, and homes. Often, it is a veiled discontent, understandably so. The mourning, the crying, the beating of chests with hands and chains, the prayers to the Imams for help, the pleas for liberation of the prisoners, and the feelings of muzzled voices all point to deep restlessness with unfulfilled dreams and incomplete lives.

However, within the beat of the life of Iran, there is the beginning of a noticeable ambivalence, not only within the avant-garde but also among the traditionally religious. Among my mullah acquaintances over a long period of time, one was adamant in his criticism of the civil religion and vowed that he would never be bought by the political establishment. He fumed and fussed about the evils of Western culture upon his countrymen and desired to return to the simple life of the village, free from the pollution and corruption of the big city. He prohibited his sons from attending cinemas. He admonished me for buying a Peykon car, as he said that most Iranians had to walk or ride the taxis and buses. However, over a period of time, this mullah bought a Volkswagen which cost double the price of a Peykon, and by the way, was a foreign model. Rather than make his annual pilgrimage to the Imam Reza Shrine in Meshed, he substituted a week-long vacation to the seacoast along the Caspian Sea. He encouraged his nephew to enroll in the Religious Corps under the auspices of the civil religion because the youth had no work at the time and would more than likely face conscription into the military service. And he began to overlook the attendance of his sons at the cinema. What a turnabout!

Another friend of mine, a young theological student, initially told me of his enthusiasm to train as a mullah in the service of his Shah and country. He spoke positively of his studies and his involvement in the religious life of the mosque, the shrine, and the many rituals which his school promoted. He dreamed of the day he might represent Iran overseas as its Islamic specialist in an embassy or consulate. He sang the praises of his king and his country. As time passed, the beat of the young man's head and heart changed. He began to despise his servitude status to his teachers, to the representatives of the regime, and to any other authority figures. He became despondent over his educational and vocational possibilities. He complained over the inadequate stipend offered, calling it a pittance and hardly enough to go to the public bath once a week. He lamented the false promises which the school made to him upon his entrance, promising him that he would be exempt from military service. Now he was told that he would have to either serve in the military service or in the Religious Corps. He had begun to study in a private night school to prepare for something other than a mullah under royal patronage. He had begun to go out into the streets without his turban and robe, substituting for them Western-styled clothing. His dreams were filled with a secure job, a wife, children, an apartment, a car, and a vacation to Europe, and even to America. What a different sound in the expectations of a young man!

The story of an unfolding Iran still has a very lively beat. Some of the clues which I heard from the sounds of daily life lived in the streets and behind the walls and in the sanctuary of declared holy places continue to vibrate in my own thinking and feeling. The Gospels depict a scene of long ago when a close disciple of Jesus

Christ followed him at a distance when Jesus faced his loneliest struggles in the trial and in the cross and in the tomb. That disciple was offbeat. That disciple at one time and place said about Jesus, "I never knew the man." It is easy to be offbeat as a foreigner in a strange land and to never know the real beat of the individual and social life of a nation. I took the risk to be immersed in the heartbeats of a people. I feel sure that more often I listened rather than spoke, sat at the steps of the mambar rather than ascended to its top, and was served more water and tea than I served. But I don't regret that. My chances for communication were as numerous as the actors and actresses in the divine-human drama in which I participated.

There is a mystery to the mazeway of the beats of life in Iran. On a hot summer's afternoon deep in the bazaar of Tehran, I ran across a silk carpeted tapestry, startling in its composition. The portraits of the Shahenshah and his Empress had been woven on the right and left sides of the carpet, and in between them there was the figure of a man with long, flowing hair. My first thought was that someone must be out of his mind to put anyone between the Shah and his consort. And then I looked for a Qur'an which would identify the face with the prophet Mohammed, and there was not one. I glanced for a sword which would say that he was Ali. But to no avail! I thought all along that it was a portrait of Jesus Christ. But that would be impossible! So I asked the owner of the shop and he confirmed that it was Jesus Christ, and would give no further details except to say, "Let it be!" And the beat goes on.